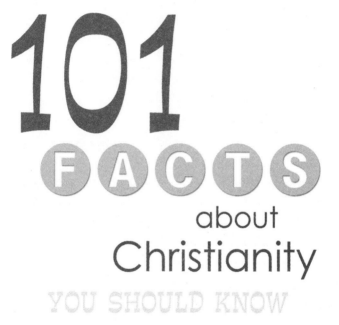

101

FACTS

about
Christianity

YOU SHOULD KNOW

Writing and compilation by Rebecca Currington, Susan Duke, Matthew Kinne, Vicki J. Kuyper, and Patricia Mitchell in association with Snapdragon Group[SM].

101

FACTS

about
Christianity

YOU SHOULD KNOW

BARBOUR
PUBLISHING

ISBN 978-1-61626-360-7

Published by Barbour Publishing, Inc., P.O. Box 719, Uhrichsville, Ohio 44683, www.barbourbooks.com

Our mission is to publish and distribute inspirational products offering exceptional value and biblical encouragement to the masses.

Member of the
Evangelical Christian
Publishers Association

Printed in the United States of Amerca.

Contents

INTRODUCTION

Methodist pastor Ralph Washington Sockman once said, "The hinge of history is on the door of a Bethlehem stable." How true! The birth of Jesus Christ changed *everything*.

The history of Christianity has been inextricably woven into the history of the world. This book, *101 Facts about Christianity You Should Know*, highlights significant Christian threads that have become part of the tapestry of world events. After reading this book, you'll walk away with an amazing overview of Christian history—the good, the bad, and, occasionally, the off-the-wall.

As you read, you'll see a bigger picture emerging, characters interacting, and events playing on and against each other. You'll see threads of compassion, martyrdom, forgiveness, hardship, courage, remembrance, accomplishment, enlightenment, and truth. You'll learn that our church history is not without blemish. Controversies, wars, and regrettable choices all prove one thing— Christians are only human, too. But you'll also see that we serve a powerful God, who moves in and through the affairs of mankind.

We hope you'll enjoy reading this book as much as we enjoyed putting it together. We've learned a lot—and you will, too. Happy reading!

THE PUBLISHERS

DIETRICH BONHOEFFER

(1906–1945)

German Pastor, Theologian, and Anti-Nazi Activist

Because German-born Dietrich Bonhoeffer was only twenty-one years old when he received his theology PhD from the University of Berlin, he was not eligible to be ordained. This gave him the opportunity to go abroad, so he spent a postgraduate year at Union Theology Seminary in New York City. There, he attended Abyssinian Baptist Church in Harlem, where he learned about social justice from the African Americans who worshipped there. Hence, when the Nazi Party took over his native homeland, he had a strong affinity for the oppressed and afflicted minorities living there.

Fact: Dietrich Bonhoeffer wrote, "When Christ calls a man, he bids him come and die."

Bonhoeffer wasn't raised in a particularly political or religious environment. He came from an aristocratic family that had nominal religious leanings. However, when Dietrich wanted to enter the ministry, his parents didn't object.

Throughout the 1930s, German pastors and theologians rallied behind Hitler, but Bonhoeffer couldn't stand the führer's anti-Semitic rhetoric. Bonhoeffer joined with like-minded theologians and launched the Confessing Church, whose members openly declared their allegiance to Jesus Christ alone. In the 1930s, he traveled to India to learn nonviolent resistance methods, and he also penned his now-famous book *The Cost of Discipleship*. He ultimately became convinced that Hitler must be removed from power, even if it meant assassinating the führer.

In 1943, Bonhoeffer was caught rescuing Jews. He was arrested and driven to Tegel Prison. Able to correspond with family and friends, he continued to write and outline his theological beliefs. Eventually, Bonhoeffer was transferred from Tegel to Buchenwald prison where he was hanged with six other resisters, just one month before Germany surrendered.

In the year 1906. . .
- Pope Pius X argued in *Vehementer Nos* against the separation of church and state.
- The *Lusitania* was launched in Glasgow.
- W. K. Kellogg founded Kellogg's, then known as the Battle Creek Toasted Corn Flake Co.

Jesus said to his disciples, "Whoever wants to be my disciple must deny themselves and take up their cross and follow me."
MATTHEW 16:24

GLADYS AYLWARD

(1902–1970)
Missionary to China

As a teenager, Gladys Aylward dreamed of traveling the world to share her faith in Jesus. She worked and saved her money, believing that God would provide an opportunity. When she was thirty years old, it came: Gladys learned of an older woman missionary in China who was seeking an assistant.

Gladys's heart must have been filled with excitement as she packed her belongings and began a long journey across England, Europe, and eastern Russia. After traveling by boat, train, bus, and mule, she arrived in Yangchen, China, and found her mentor, Mrs. Larson. The missionary and a Christian Chinese cook were ministering at an inn for muleteers. Gladys gladly joined them as they shared food, shelter, Bible teaching, and God's love.

Fact: Gladys's march to Sian with her bevy of orphans became a film—*Inn of the Sixth Happiness,* starring Ingrid Bergman—in 1958. However, Gladys was upset that screenwriters fabricated a love interest—a Eurasian soldier—for her character.

After Mrs. Larson died, Gladys settled in Yangchen. She learned the language and immersed herself in the culture. Eventually she became a Chinese citizen and was well known to the local Chinese officials. Quietly and faithfully, Gladys worked with the city's prisoners and lepers.

When the Japanese attacked China in World War II, Gladys fled Yangchen for shelter in Sian with one hundred orphans in tow. After a nerve-racking, twelve-day journey through the mountains, the group was halted by the Yellow River, with no way to cross. A Chinese officer, who heard Gladys and the children praying and singing, arranged a boat for their crossing.

A simple teenage girl with a heart's desire to share her faith played an extraordinary role in the evangelization of the nation of China. Gladys Aylward's story is immortalized in the book *The Small Woman* by Alan Burgess.

In the year 1902...
- Andrew Carnegie founded the Carnegie Institution.
- Theodore Roosevelt successfully negotiated with miners in the Anthracite Coal Strike.
- The Second Boer War ended with the Treaty of Vereeniging.

"And everyone who has left houses or brothers or sisters or father or mother or wife or children or fields for my sake will receive a hundred times as much and will inherit eternal life."
MATTHEW 19:29

THE CATACOMBS

Rome

Though underground cemeteries have been found throughout Asia Minor, Egypt, Tunisia, and Malta, the word *catacombs* has become almost synonymous with the funereal tunnels of Rome. This maze of galleries and chambers, up to five levels deep, was carved out of the soft volcanic rock outside the city walls of Rome. (Burials were not allowed within the city walls.) Forty different catacombs have been discovered in the environs of Rome, one as recently as 1959.

Both Christians and Jews, who did not believe in cremation like many Romans did, were buried here. Rectangular niches, called *loculi*, line the narrow passageways of the Roman catacombs. The bodies of canonized saints, martyrs, clergy, as well as common citizens, were wrapped in linen, placed in sarcophagi, and then slid into these niches. The loculi were then sealed with stone slabs. The walls of the catacombs were decorated with brilliant-colored frescoes, the most popular subject being Jesus' raising Lazarus from the dead.

Fact: Contrary to popular belief, early Roman Christians did not use the catacombs as a hiding place from those persecuting them. That's just a story line from novels and film.

Despite the persecution of Christians during the first three centuries, the Romans held these catacombs as sacrosanct and did not disturb them. On occasion, Christians gathered there to celebrate Communion or the anniversary of someone's death. In the seventh century, visiting the catacombs became a popular pilgrimage for European Christians. The catacombs were even part of an ancient *itineraria*, or tourist guidebook, describing the sacred sites of Rome. However, by the tenth century most of the bones had been moved to churches for veneration as relics. Soon after, the tombs were all but forgotten.

In the year 1959. . .
• The Dalai Lama sought asylum in India after fleeing Tibet.
• Fidel Castro gained power in Cuba.
• The sci-fi television series *The Twilight Zone* premiered.

> *Jesus said to her, "I am the resurrection and the life.*
> *The one who believes in me will live, even though they die."*
> JOHN 11:25

4

THE AZUSA STREET REVIVAL

Outpouring of the Holy Spirit

The fire of the Holy Spirit fell on us." That's the picture painted by those attending the Azusa Street Revival, which took place in Los Angeles in the early 1900s.

William J. Seymour, an African American preacher, became pastor of the Azusa Street Mission in April 1906. The mission was nothing more than an abandoned church building with apartments upstairs and a stable for horses below. It measured about forty by sixty feet.

Fact: Some observers told newspaper reporters that God's presence was so heavy on the Azusa Street Mission that people were knocked to the ground blocks from the mission building itself.

Seymour, whose preaching stressed the gifts of the Holy Spirit, gave special attention to speaking in tongues (or *glossolalia*) as a sign that believers had been baptized in the Holy Spirit. The worship was devout and intense. People "fell back" under the power of God, and at times, worshippers would break into spontaneous singing in unscripted harmonies. Some claimed miracles and healings.

For the next three and a half years, the crowds continued to visit Azusa Street, staying around the clock despite the hot, smelly, fly-infested surroundings. As many as fifteen hundred people reportedly jammed the old stable, covering windows and doors and stifling every trace of a breeze. But the worshippers were undeterred.

Some claimed the meetings seemed to run themselves while

Seymour knelt, deeply engrossed in prayer. The revival was multi-racial and multidenominational and featured the poor and women prominently. Many who visited Azusa Street carried the flame of revival back to their own congregations, starting the modern Pentecostal movement.

In the year 1906. . .
- The 1906 San Francisco earthquake struck along the San Andreas Fault.
- Gandhi introduced his idea of nonviolent resistance.
- The Victor Talking Machine Company manufactured the first Victor-Victrola phonograph.

[Jesus said,] "You will receive power when the Holy Spirit comes on you; and you will be my witnesses in Jerusalem, and in all Judea and Samaria, and to the ends of the earth."
ACTS 1:8

5

BEN-HUR: A TALE OF THE CHRIST

By General Lew Wallace (1880)

Categorized as historical fiction, *Ben-Hur: A Tale of the Christ* was a phenomenal success, quickly surpassing Harriet Beecher Stowe's *Uncle Tom's Cabin* as the bestselling American novel. It remained so until the publication of Margaret Mitchell's *Gone with the Wind* in 1936.

Ben-Hur is a tale of betrayal, revenge, and salvation that provides a credible glimpse into the geography and culture of the ancient world. The story concerns the life of Judah Ben-Hur, a rich Jewish prince and merchant in first-century Jerusalem. One day he encounters a childhood friend, Messala, who is now a commanding officer of a Roman legion. At first the two are glad to see each other, but eventually they clash over political issues. Messala betrays Judah, and the young prince is forced to serve as a galley slave on a ship, while his mother and sister are imprisoned. Upon Judah's release, he seeks revenge, taking on his betrayer in a wild chariot race in which Messala is mortally wounded. Only after Judah encounters Jesus and witnesses His crucifixion does he find redemption and forgiveness.

Fact: No proof has been produced, but some believe MGM covered up the death of a stuntman in the 1959 movie version of Ben-Hur—and kept the fatal, chariot scene accident in the film.

This book has been adapted for both stage and film. After *Ben-Hur*'s release in 1880, it became a Broadway play in 1899. Silent film versions were made in 1907 and 1925—the most expensive silent film ever made. In 1959, the feature film starring Charlton

Heston was released—the most expensive color film of its time and the first to win eleven Oscars. A musical version was released in 1999, followed by an animated film in 2003 with Charlton Heston as the voice of Ben-Hur.

In the year 1880. . .
- Workers finished construction on Cologne Cathedral that had begun in 1248.
- James Garfield won the U.S. presidential election against Winfield Hancock.
- Thomas Edison received Patent No. 223,898 for his electric lamp.

Bear with each other and forgive one another if any of you has a grievance against someone. Forgive as the Lord forgave you.
COLOSSIANS 3:13

6

"A Mighty Fortress Is Our God"

Words and Music by Martin Luther (1529)
Translated into English by Frederic H. Hedge (1853)

This thunderous, weighty hymn just seems to demand respect. A paraphrase of Psalm 46:1, it is the most well known of Luther's hymns and the best loved of the Lutheran and Protestant traditions. It has even been called "The Battle Hymn of the Reformation."

Fact: This song has been called "the greatest hymn of the greatest man of the greatest period of German history."

In actuality the original melody for this hymn differs dramatically from what congregations sing in most Protestant churches. Described as extremely rhythmic, it bends to all the nuances of the text. Around the time the hymn was translated into English, some disputed Luther's authorship. Since then, however, it has been clearly established that Luther did compose the tune to go with the lyrics he had written earlier.

Tradition has it that Luther and his companions sang this hymn as they marched into the city of Worms in 1521 for the Diet of Worms, an assembly best known for addressing Luther's *Ninety-Five Theses* and the Protestant Reformation.

A mighty fortress is our God, a bulwark never failing;
Our helper He, amid the flood of mortal ills prevailing:
For still our ancient foe doth seek to work us woe;
His craft and power are great, and, armed with cruel hate,
On earth is not his equal.

That word above all earthly powers, no thanks to them, abideth;
The Spirit and the gifts are ours through Him who with us sideth:
Let goods and kindred go, this mortal life also;
The body they may kill: God's truth abideth still,
His kingdom is forever.

In the year 1529. . .
- Spain and Portugal decided on a division of the eastern hemisphere in the Treaty of Saragossa.
- Archbishop of York, Thomas Wolsey, resigned after failing to secure a divorce for Henry VIII.
- Turkish forces under Sultan Suleiman attempted to capture Vienna but ultimately failed.

God is our refuge and strength,
an ever-present help in trouble.
PSALM 46:1

APOLLO 8

Moon Mission

On December 24, 1968, an estimated one quarter of the earth's population heard the Bible's account of Creation, thanks to astronauts of the Apollo 8 mission. Mission commander Frank Borman, command module pilot James Lovell, and lunar module pilot William Anders used the occasion of a live television broadcast from space to read Genesis 1:1–10 (KJV):

Fact: Famed atheist Madalyn Murray O'Hair filed suit against NASA to ban federal employees from such public "prayers." Courts eventually denied her argument.

In the beginning God created the heaven and the earth.

And the earth was without form, and void; and darkness was upon the face of the deep. And the Spirit of God moved upon the face of the waters.

And God said, Let there be light: and there was light.

And God saw the light, that it was good: and God divided the light from the darkness.

And God called the light Day, and the darkness he called Night. And the evening and the morning were the first day.

And God said, Let there be a firmament in the midst of the waters, and let it divide the waters from the waters.

And God made the firmament, and divided the waters which were under the firmament from the waters which were above the firmament: and it was so.

And God called the firmament Heaven. And the evening

and the morning were the second day.

And God said, Let the waters under the heaven be gathered together unto one place, and let the dry land appear: and it was so.

And God called the dry land Earth; and the gathering together of the waters called he Seas: and God saw that it was good.

Apollo 8's primary mission was to circle the moon (which the astronauts did ten times over twenty hours), scouting Earth's satellite for the planned lunar landing of the Apollo 11 mission. Borman's team took numerous photographs of the moon as well as the Earth—including the first image of the "earthrise," a dramatic view of our planet never seen before.

The orbiting Genesis reading thrilled some. Borman said later that Pope Paul VI told him, "I have spent my entire life trying to say to the world what you did on Christmas Eve."

In the year 1968. . .
- Civil rights leader Martin Luther King Jr. was killed in Tennessee.
- Workers and students united in Paris to protest their government in a movement called May '68.
- Great Britain experimented with a year-round system of daylight saving time.

Since the creation of the world God's invisible qualities—his eternal power and divine nature—have been clearly seen, being understood from what has been made, so that people are without excuse.
ROMANS 1:20

JOHN BUNYAN

(1628–1688)
Author of The Pilgrim's Progress

Despite creating such a beloved, often-translated Christian allegorical work as *The Pilgrim's Progress*, British author John Bunyan faced a life of difficulty and obstacles. First, he had little schooling. His formal education lasted only two to four years; he served as an apprentice in his father's tinker's trade, and he also spent some time in military service. Second, his youth appeared not to be one of piety, but of abandonment, where he indulged in profanity and other behaviors considered sinful at the time. For a while, he was racked with fear over having committed the "unpardonable sin." Some even believe he suffered psychotic illnesses. Only after becoming an enthusiastic believer while immersing himself in the Baptist Church did he feel free from his mental and spiritual burdens.

Fact: Sir Walter Scott believed John Bunyan was of gypsy descent because his father was a traveling tinker—a mender of pots and pans. Others say the elder Bunyan was a village blacksmith.

These trials became the basis for his great work *The Pilgrim's Progress*. As he began to write, he also preached, and this, too, became a contentious issue in his life. He fiercely disagreed with the Quakers and at one point was indicted for preaching without a license. When he refused to stop preaching, he was thrown into prison. For twelve years he was confined, and there he wrote a large part of his definitive work. Only after Charles II issued the Declaration of Religious Indulgence was Bunyan finally released. But Bunyan began to preach again, causing Charles II to retract his declaration and throw Bunyan into prison again. Despite these circumstances, Bunyan was able to finish his masterpiece.

An uneducated, mentally anguished criminal wrote *The Pilgrim's Progress*, the second-most translated book of all time behind the Bible.

In the year 1628. . .
• Puritans from the Massachusetts Bay Colony arrived in Salem, Massachusetts.
• The English Parliament's Petition of Right outlined the offences of Charles I.
• The Battle of Wolgast marked the end of Danish involvement in the Thirty Years' War.

Give your burdens to the LORD, and he will take care of you.
He will not permit the godly to slip and fall.
PSALM 55:22 NLT

CATHERINE BOOTH

(1829–1890)
Female Preacher, Activist,
and Cofounder of the Salvation Army

Catherine Mumford was born in Ashbourne, Derbyshire, in 1829. By the time she was twelve, she had read through the Bible eight times. Catherine first glimpsed her call to social justice when she stood up for a drunken man she felt had been mistreated by a local policeman.

In 1852, Catherine met William Booth, a Methodist minister. While they shared the same view on social reform, Catherine highly objected to William's nonfeminist views on women, especially a woman's role in the church and her right to preach. Despite their differences, Catherine and William married on June 16, 1855.

One morning in 1860 at Gateshead Bethseda Chapel, Catherine recalled, she suddenly felt compelled to stand up and speak. She found herself preaching her first sermon, and it so impressed her husband that he changed his mind about women preachers. Catherine soon gained a reputation as an extraordinary speaker and began preaching revivals at London's Christian Mission, which later became the Salvation Army.

Fact: Catherine Booth died of cancer in October 1890. She and William Booth had eight children, all of whom were active in the Salvation Army.

When the Church of England called William Booth the antichrist for elevating women to a man's status, William answered his accusers, "The best men in my army are the women."

In 1882, a London survey reported that on one weeknight, there were almost seventeen thousand worshipping with the Salvation Army compared to eleven thousand in mainline churches.

Catherine's tireless campaigns for social reform included organizing Food-for-the-Million Shops, where the poor could buy affordable meals; cooking Christmas Day dinners to feed the poor; waging war on match factories that presented health risks from unsafe chemicals; and fearlessly fighting for better wages for women.

In the year 1829. . .
- Religious freedom was restored in Ireland.
- Britain abolished *sati*, the Indian custom of a widow burning herself on a funeral pyre.
- Gioacchino Rossini's opera *William Tell* premiered.

Dear children, let us not love with words
or speech but with actions and in truth.
1 JOHN 3:18

ENFIELD, CONNECTICUT

Epicenter of the Great Awakening

Along the Eastern seaboard in the early 1700s, the fledgling British colonies were quickly sliding away from their religious roots. Many people lived on small farms or plantations miles away from their neighbors. Church membership dropped as families became more self-sufficient and didn't want to travel a long distance to attend church. Among the dwindling group of still-staunch Puritans, there was concern that the younger generation was becoming too "frivolous" and that morality was on a downhill slide. Then a wave of religious fervor rolled over the colonies. It became known as the "Great Awakening." Enfield, Connecticut, was at the epicenter of the revival.

In July of 1741, Calvinist Congregationalist minister Jonathan Edwards traveled to Enfield to preach at a local church. He'd previously preached "Sinners in the Hands of an Angry God" at his own church in Northampton, Massachusetts, with little response. But the Enfield church was different.

Fact: Due to a surveyor's error, Enfield was originally settled as part of the colony of Massachusetts.

When people heard Edwards (who has been described as "monotone" and "boring") preach on Deuteronomy 32:35, their emotional response to his "fire and brimstone" message was overwhelming. People wept, swooned, went into convulsions, and even barked like dogs. So many people committed their lives to God that Edwards preached the sermon several times. His words were also printed and distributed around the countryside.

As a result, a revival took place throughout the churches of New England.

Today, "Sinners in the Hands of an Angry God" is frequently used in high school and college English classes as a classic example of Puritan literature.

In the year 1741...
• The New York Slave Conspiracy resulted in numerous executions of black slaves.
• Elizabeth of Russia took power in the Palace Revolution of 1741.
• Danish explorer Vitus Bering discovered Alaska.

"It is mine to avenge; I will repay. In due time their foot will slip; their day of disaster is near and their doom rushes upon them."
DEUTERONOMY 32:35

11

BILLY GRAHAM'S
LOS ANGELES CRUSADE

In November of 1949, a little-known Baptist evangelist pitched a tent over a sawdust floor in downtown Los Angeles. His planned three-week revival lasted more than eight weeks.

The dynamic young preacher, Billy Graham, enthralled his hearers and caught the attention of William Randolph Hearst, the newspaper magnate. As a result, Hearst newspapers nationwide published Billy Graham headlines and photos. Graham's decades-long career was launched.

Fact: Billy Graham said, "My one purpose in life is to help people find a personal relationship with God, which, I believe, comes through knowing Christ."

Graham's crusades continued to draw large to overflowing crowds and were routinely extended. A crusade in London lasted nearly three months, and one in New York City ran nightly for four months. Graham, who has held crusades in 185 countries and territories, has preached to more live audiences than anyone else in history. Through his radio broadcasts, televised crusades, films, webcasts, books, and magazines, Graham has reached untold millions of souls with the gospel of Jesus Christ.

Graham holds a unique place among evangelists. He has achieved prominence, respect, and influence in a variety of secular and religious spheres. U.S. presidents have invited him to the White House on numerous occasions. The evangelist has received awards from a range of organizations and honorary doctorates from institutions in the U.S. and abroad.

In November of 2004, fifty-five years after the sawdust-floor tent meetings in downtown Los Angeles, Graham held another crusade, this time at the 92,000-seat Rose Bowl in neighboring Pasadena. The four-day event drew 312,500 people to hear Graham preach, and more than 14,000 of them committed their lives to Jesus Christ.

In the year 1949. . .
• The People's Republic of China was established on October 1.
• Harry S Truman formally introduced his Fair Deal program.
• Clothes rationing ended in Britain.

You have been born again, not of perishable seed, but of imperishable,
through the living and enduring word of God.
1 PETER 1:23

12

THE BOOK OF MARTYRS

By John Foxe (1563)

Lavishly produced and illustrated with a number of woodcuts, *The Book of Martyrs* provides accounts of the persecutions of Protestant Christians—most from England. The first part of the book deals with early Christian martyrs; the second with those persecuted under the reigns of Henry VIII and Edward VI; the third with the reign of Mary Tudor—Bloody Mary, as some have referred to her.

Since many of the victims of these poignant stories are listed in official registers only with name and occupation, no corroborating documentation exists. This has caused some historians to question the accuracy of Foxe's claims. That certainly didn't keep the book from becoming a favorite with readers, however. It was especially popular with Puritans and low church families, probably because of its intense style and colorful dialogues. Before long it was—along with the Bible—being chained to the lectern in churches, where it would be accessible to the people.

Fact: The original *Book of Martyrs* was enormous—2,300 pages—and the largest publishing project completed in England until that time.

Though the work is commonly known as *Foxe's Book of Martyrs*, the full title is *Actes and Monuments of these Latter and Perillous Days, Touching Matters of the Church.* Foxe based his book not only on documents and reports of the trials but also on personal accounts of friends and families of the martyrs. Although Foxe reported all that was told him, many feel he was purposely misled at times, even by some who wished to discredit his work. Four large volumes were printed just in the author's lifetime, and the book continues to have great influence to this day.

In the year 1563. . .
- The Council of Trent ended (it began in 1545), reaffirming Roman Catholic doctrine.
- Charles VI ordered all Jews expelled from France.
- The Duke of Guise died while taking Orléans.

Be faithful, even to the point of death,
and I will give you life as your victor's crown.
REVELATION 2:10

13

"AMAZING GRACE"

Words by John Newton (1779)
Music by James P. Carrel and David S. Clayton (1831)

John Newton's devoutly religious mother died just before he turned seven years old. By age eleven, he'd joined this father's ship in hopes of becoming a seaman. He later served on other ships and bore the reputation of being quite rebellious and immoral. When he worked on the islands and mainland of West Africa, he witnessed the cruelty of slavery firsthand, and became the captain of his own slave ship, transporting slaves to America.

Fact: The last stanza, which begins, "When we've been there ten thousand years," was added by an unknown author and appeared as early as 1829.

On March 10, 1748, after a close brush with death during a particularly stormy voyage back to England, John began reading a book by a Dutch monk, Thomas à Kempis, called *Imitation of Christ*. The book and his experience greatly influenced his eventual conversion to Christianity.

John studied for ministry and was ordained by the Anglican Church. He served as pastor near Cambridge, England, and held additional services in larger venues where people enthusiastically gathered to hear the story of his conversion.

John began writing hymns when he couldn't find enough simple and heartfelt congregational songs as opposed to the staid and more formal hymns of the Anglican Church. Through his hymn "Amazing Grace," he continues to share his testimony of God's grace in his life. Today, it is arguably the most popular hymn in the English language.

> *Amazing grace! How sweet the sound*
> *That saved a wretch like me!*
> *I once was lost, but now am found;*
> *Was blind, but now I see.*

In the year 1779. . .
- Spain declared war on England, joining the U.S. forces in the American Revolutionary War.
- Navigator James Cook died while exploring the Sandwich Islands.
- The first cast-iron bridge, known as the Iron Bridge, was finished.

> *"I was blind but now I see!"*
> JOHN 9:25

BIKERS FOR CHRIST

Christian Motorcycle Clubs

Drivers of a certain age may still shudder to see a swarm of motorcycles pull up beside them at a stoplight. In the 1950s, you would have prayed for a fast getaway, your head reeling with lurid newspaper stories of biker mayhem. Now you're likely to glance over and see riders you recognize—from your church.

Local motorcycling organizations formed in the early years of the twentieth century. In 1924, the American Motorcyclist Association (AMA) was founded by motorcycle manufacturers to promote riding among the general public. The AMA supported rider clubs with national fellowship events, rider education programs, and public relations.

Christian biker clubs got on the road in the 1970s as motorcycling went mainstream. Clubs formed among local Christian riders (many of whom were ministers) to promote fellowship, hone riding skills, and spread the gospel in the biking community. Groups identified themselves by wearing T-shirts or jacket patches sporting a Bible verse, cross, or praying hands. Many clubs sponsored community food and clothing drives and took their ministry to shelters, jails, and even among "hard-core" bikers—those you *don't* want to see in the rearview mirror.

Fact: *The Wild One*, a 1953 movie based on a biker gathering gone awry, reinforced a negative public view of motorcyclists. In response, the AMA wrote to condemn the "1 percent" who belonged to outlaw clubs.

The Christian Motorcyclists

Association (CMA), in existence since the 1970s, now claims more than one hundred thousand members nationally and internationally. Soldiers for Jesus and Bikers for Christ are also large international ministries that organize Christian bikers around a wide range of community and charitable activities. The Christian club associations routinely screen applicants, often requiring references and a waiting period before granting membership. Their consistently positive press has earned Christian bikers widespread respect and admiration.

In the year 1975. . .
- The Helsinki Accords were signed to promote continued stability in Europe.
- Junko Tabei became the first woman to reach Mt. Everest's summit.
- Robert E. Lee's citizenship was restored posthumously.

In your majesty ride forth victoriously in
the cause of truth, humility and justice.
PSALM 45:4

Oswald Chambers

(1874–1917)
Author of *My Utmost for His Highest*

One of Christianity's most beloved devotional authors, Oswald Chambers, originally found God's Word unimpressive. Born in Scotland to devout Baptist parents in 1874, he described the Bible at Dunoon College as "dull and uninspiring." He, instead, gravitated toward the works of Robert Browning, even starting a study society dedicated to exploring this poet.

Fact: The only book that Oswald Chambers actually penned is given the enigmatic moniker *Baffled to Fight Better*.

After four years of spiritual emptiness, Chambers ultimately came to the conclusion that he couldn't make himself holy. He eventually realized that only Christ could redeem him from his depravity and give him strength and peace. Chambers was then born anew into a condition he described as a "radiant, unspeakable emancipation." Those who knew him said he was fond of saying, "Beware of reasoning about God's Word—obey it."

In 1908, on board a ship bound for America, Chambers met Gertrude "Biddy" Hobbs, a stenographer, who would become his wife two years later. Together, they ran the Bible Training College in Clapham, London. After only a few years, Chambers suspended operations at the college because he believed he should serve as a chaplain during World War I. He was stationed in Egypt.

Oswald Chambers died as a result of a ruptured appendix in 1917 in Egypt. He endured the pain of appendicitis for three days before seeking medical help because he didn't want to take a hospital bed needed by a wounded soldier. Biddy announced his passing with a simple telegram, OSWALD; IN HIS PRESENCE.

In the year 1874. . .
• Gold was discovered in the Dakota Territory, beginning the Black Hills Gold Rush.
• German archaeologist Heinrich Schliemann excavated the remains of Mycenae in Greece.
• The United States' first public zoo opened in Philadelphia, Pennsylvania.

[Jesus said,] "The one who speaks on his own authority seeks his own glory; but the one who seeks the glory of him who sent him is true, and in him there is no falsehood."
JOHN 7:18 ESV

G. K. CHESTERTON

(1874–1936)
English Writer of Christian Apologetics

A large and jovial man, writer G. K. Chesterton often exercised verbal sparring with his friends and fellow academics. Once while talking with George Bernard Shaw, Chesterton said, "To look at you, anyone would think there was a famine in England."

Shaw retorted, "To look at you, anyone would think you caused it."

Born in London, Chesterton was initially educated to be an artist. He produced paintings and illustrations throughout his writing career. Misunderstood and labeled controversial, he often wrote paradoxes like the phrase, "Anything worth doing is worth doing badly." He believed that such turns of speech were an excellent vehicle for communicating great truth. None of his works gained prominence as a definitive work, but various writings (or the entire collection) influenced such luminaries as Mahatma Ghandi, George Orwell, T. S. Eliot, and C. S. Lewis. In fact, his Christian apologetics were instrumental in Lewis's conversion.

Fact: G. K. Chesterton said, "The Bible tells us to love our neighbors and also to love our enemies, probably because they are generally the same people."

Though he was raised in the Church of England, he called himself an "orthodox Christian." Later in life, as he became more and more comfortable with Catholicism, he converted to the Church of Rome.

Not long after writing his autobiography, Chesterton fell ill and died. Following his funeral, Pope

Pius XI declared Chesterton "Defender of the Faith—a title as true for Protestants as it is for Catholics."

Chesterton wrote about eighty books, several hundred poems, two hundred short stories, four thousand essays, and several plays. He wrote the biography of *Charles Dickens* (1903), and authored works such as *The Man Who Was Thursday* (1907), *Orthodoxy* (1908), and the *Father Brown* short stories.

In the year 1874. . .
• India's Agra Canal opened.
• Iceland received a constitution and the right to limited home rule from Denmark.
• Thomas Nast used an elephant to represent the Republican Party in a *Harper's Weekly* cartoon.

[Jesus said,] "I say, love your enemies!
Pray for those who persecute you!"
MATTHEW 5:44 NLT

Amy Carmichael

(1867–1951)

Missionary to India / Founder of Dohnavur Fellowship

The oldest of seven children, Amy Carmichael was born December 16, 1867, in Millisle, Northern Ireland, to devout Presbyterian parents. When her father died in 1885, she was adopted and tutored by Robert Wilson, founder of the Keswick Convention.

Fact: A prolific writer, Amy Carmichael produced thirty-five published books including *His Thoughts Said. . .His Father Said* (1951), *If* (1953), and *Edges of His Ways* (1955).

As a child Amy was considered tomboyish and poetic. She never married. After hearing Hudson Taylor speak at the Keswick Convention in 1887 about missionary life, Amy was convinced her life's calling was to the mission field. Despite a nerve disease and severe weakness in her body that often required complete bed rest, Amy was committed to her calling.

In 1892, after hearing the words, "Go ye," Amy fully believed she was ready to serve in the mission field; but the China Inland Mission rejected her as a missionary because of her physical frailty. Regardless of the report, Robert Wilson sent her to Japan as a Keswick missionary. Within that first year, Amy's health problems worsened. During times of great physical weakness, when she felt like a failure as a missionary, Amy remained dedicated to her calling.

Commissioned by the Church of England's Zenana Missionary Society in 1895, she arrived in India, where she found her lifelong vocation and remained for fifty-six years. She was dedicated to saving many young women from forced prostitution. She also founded Dohnavur Fellowship in Tamil Naduto, a sanctuary and rescue mission for hopeless, suffering children. Selflessness, commitment, and an example of one whose sole existence was devoted to her beloved Lord and Savior were the marks of Amy Carmichael's life.

In the year 1867...
- Nebraska became the thirty-seventh state of the United States.
- Karl Marx and Friedrich Engels published the first of three volumes of *Das Kapital*.
- Emperor Meiji took power in Japan.

"Therefore go and make disciples of all nations."
MATTHEW 28:19

THE JORDAN RIVER

Northern Israel

In the Old Testament, the Jordan River was the site of several miracles. In the book of Joshua, the flow of the river stopped to allow the Israelites, and the priests who carried the ark of the covenant, to cross. In 2 Kings, God empowered Elijah to stop the river's flow with a touch of his cloak, heal an army commander of leprosy by having him wash in the Jordan, and made an iron ax head float on the river's surface. But the main reason people consider the Jordan River sacred is because it's the site of Jesus' baptism, recorded in the New Testament.

Fact: No swimming, fishing, picnicking, or boating is allowed in the area surrounding Yardenit.

More than four hundred thousand visitors a year travel from all over the world to Yardenit—the spot where the Jordan flows out of the Sea of Galilee—to follow Jesus' example. A visitors' center, held up by huge pillars in the shape of a cross, houses a souvenir shop resembling a Galilean-style bazaar. Here visitors can rent white baptismal robes and towels, pick up a certificate of baptism or rededication, or purchase a Jesus-shaped bottle to bring home water from the River Jordan, 364 days a year. (Yardenit is closed only on the Jewish holiday of Yom Kippur.) Participants can choose to be baptized by immersion or have a pastor or priest sprinkle them with water from a tree branch dipped into the river.

Other than the relatively clean water flowing through the Yardenit region (thanks to a nearby dam and hydraulic plant), today the remaining two hundred miles of the Jordan River is stagnant and polluted.

In the first century. . .
• Thomas the Apostle brought Christian teachings to India.
• Rome's first emperor, Augustus Caesar, died.
• The Colosseum was built in Rome.

*Then Jesus came from Galilee to
the Jordan to be baptized by John.*
MATTHEW 3:13

19

THE CIVIL RIGHTS MARCH ON WASHINGTON, DC

Before the 1960s, race sharply divided American towns and cities. Certain neighborhoods, schools, businesses, and churches were "white" and others "black." White home buyers in the fifties might remember a clause in their deeds that forbade the sale of their home to blacks.

Fact: One of Dr. King's early demonstrations led to his arrest and his "Letter from Birmingham Jail." In it, King argued for the moral right of citizens to disobey unjust laws.

Things began to change when Dr. Martin Luther King Jr. emerged on the public scene. The son of a minister and a minister himself, King challenged racial segregation and the oppression of blacks. In 1957, he was one of the founding members of the Southern Christian Leadership Conference (SCLC) and the organization's most prominent speaker and fund-raiser. Strongly influenced by Indian leader Mahatma Gandhi, King espoused nonviolent protest and persuasion to change the entrenched injustice of American racism.

On August 28, 1963, King, along with other black leaders, led a demonstration in Washington, DC for jobs and civil rights. King roused the crowd of two hundred fifty thousand with an eloquent address, his "I Have a Dream Speech." In his signature soaring oratorical style, King encapsulated the hopes of all oppressed Americans: "I have a dream that one day this nation will rise up and live out the true meaning of its creed: 'We hold these truths to be self-evident, that all men are created equal. . . .' I have a dream that my four little children will one day live in a nation where they will not be judged by the color of their skin, but by the content of their character."

The Civil Rights Act, prohibiting segregation in public places and discrimination in education and employment, was passed in 1964. King was awarded the 1964 Nobel Prize for peace.

In the year 1963. . .
• John F. Kennedy was assassinated.
• Alcatraz Island Federal Penitentiary closed.
• Kenya gained independence from the United Kingdom.

> *This is what the LORD says: "Maintain justice and do what is right, for my salvation is close at hand and my righteousness will soon be revealed."*
> ISAIAH 56:1

20

BORN AGAIN

By Charles "Chuck" W. Colson (1976)

That the president's powerful and influential "hatchet man" would end up in a prison cell surprises no one these days. In the decades since the Watergate debacle of the Nixon administration, we've seen one high-profile scandal after another. But that a formerly ruthless operative would emerge to prominence as a born-again Christian and humanitarian deserves notice.

During his four years of service to President Nixon, even the most powerful politicians feared Charles Colson, the president's "hatchet man." Colson had been willing to do just about anything for his political party and the president, including trying to cover up the burglary at the center of the Watergate scandal.

> Fact: Chuck Colson wrote, "All I knew was that I had a story I must tell, a story that might bring hope and encouragement to others."

In *Born Again*, Charles "Chuck" Colson relates how, as Watergate investigations were unraveling the workings of the Nixon administration and revealing his illegal actions as special counsel to the president, he was thrown into a torturous search for hope and strength. In the office of a friend, he fell into tears of repentance. His friend prayed over him, and Colson, for the first time in his life, experienced the presence of God. At his trial, he pleaded guilty to obstruction of justice and was sentenced to one to three years as a guest of the U.S. government.

Colson was the first of the Nixon administration to go to prison for charges related to the Watergate scandal. He served seven months of his sentence, using his prison time to study the

Bible, pray, and write the notes that became his autobiography, *Born Again*. The book was made into a movie of the same name in 1978.

In the year 1976. . .
- On July 4, the United States celebrated its bicentennial as a country.
- Military forces suppressed protestors at Tiananmen Square in Beijing, China.
- The "Cod" Wars between the United Kingdom and Iceland ended.

"But you, LORD my God,
brought my life up from the pit."
JONAH 2:6

21

"BE THOU MY VISION"

Words by Dallan Forgaill (Sixth Century)
Music: Irish Folk Song: "Slane" (Unknown)

Considered the quintessential Irish hymn sung in English-speaking churches, "Be Thou My Vision" has been part of Irish monastic tradition for centuries.

Dallan Forgaill, thought to be the author of the lyrics, was a sixth-century monk martyred in 598 by pirates who invaded the island monastery where he lived. During his life, he was widely known as the chief poet of Ireland. Tradition has it that Forgaill studied so intently that he became blind from reading and writing poetry.

Fact: "Be Thou My Vision" has become a popular song performed by contemporary Christian musicians such as Rebecca St. James, Ginny Owens, and Jars of Clay.

The text of the hymn was translated from Old Irish into English by Mary E. Byrne in 1905. Oddly, she chose to keep the Elizabethan language. "Be Thou My Vision" is sung to the Irish folk song, "Slane," which tells the story of Slane Hill, where in AD 433 St. Patrick lit candles on Easter Eve in defiance of the pagan king Loe-gaire.

The context of the hymn is a prayer proclaiming Christ as our model and ideal. Each stanza begins with an aspect of His provision as: my vision, my wisdom, my true word, my great Father, my inheritance, my treasure, and my heart of my heart. The first and last stanzas are given here.

Be Thou my Vision, O Lord of my heart;
Nought be all else to me, save that Thou art.
Thou my best Thought, by day or by night,
Waking or sleeping, Thy presence my light.

High King of Heaven, my victory won,
May I reach Heaven's joys, O bright Heaven's Sun!
Heart of my own heart, whatever befall,
Still be my Vision, O Ruler of all.

In the year 1905. . .
- The Treaty of Portsmouth ended the Russo-Japanese War.
- The union between Norway and Sweden dissolved.
- The Cullinan diamond—weighing over 3,000 carats—was discovered in South Africa.

My eyes are fixed on you, Sovereign LORD;
in you I take refuge.
PSALM 141:8

CHARIOTS OF FIRE

The Eric Liddell Story (1981)

"God made me fast, and when I run, I feel His pleasure." While Eric Liddell's quote from the film *Chariots of Fire* describes delight only a dedicated runner could relate to, the story has captured the hearts of diverse audiences for over twenty-five years. The British film won an Oscar for Best Picture in 1981 and numerous other awards.

Chariots of Fire is based on the experiences of Harold Abrahams and Eric Liddell, two Cambridge University undergraduates who competed in the 1924 Paris Summer Olympics. Abrahams, a nonreligious Jew, overcame anti-Semitism and proved himself an exceptional sprinter. His nearest competitor was Eric Liddell, also an exceptional sprinter. The story follows the two athletes and contrasts their motivations to compete and win. Abrahams ran to achieve the acceptance and status winning would confer on him. Liddell ran for the God-given pleasure of running. Win or lose, he planned to leave for his father's mission in China upon graduation.

Fact: William Blake penned the line, "Bring me my chariot of fire," in the poem "Jerusalem" from his epic work *Milton*.

Liddell resolved not to run on Sunday in honor of the Sabbath. This meant he couldn't run in a race in which he excelled. He ran another race on another day instead. In the movie, Abrahams won but found no lasting satisfaction in his victory, while Liddell discovered joy not dependent on winning, but on being faithful to the dictates of his religion and following God's purpose for his life.

While the screenplay contains several inaccuracies of fact

and circumstance, it tells compellingly the real story of Liddell's struggles and perseverance. The film's stirring music and uplifting themes of resolve, integrity, and character along with its Christian message continue to resonate with viewers.

In the year 1981. . .
- Sandra Day O'Connor was appointed to the Supreme Court, becoming the first female member.
- Broadcast journalist Walter Cronkite retired from his work on the *CBS Evening News*.
- Charles, Prince of Wales married Lady Diana Spencer at St. Paul's Cathedral.

Those who hope in the LORD will renew their strength. They will soar on wings like eagles; they will run and not grow weary, they will walk and not be faint.
ISAIAH 40:31

FREDERICK DOUGLASS

(1818–1895)
American Abolitionist and Statesman

Born a slave in Talbot County, Maryland, Frederick Douglass was separated from his mother while still an infant and raised as an orphan. However, his slave master's wife took an interest in him. Noticing his obvious intellectual promise, she broke the law and taught him the alphabet. From there, young Frederick learned to read by watching the white children around him.

Fact: Frederick Douglass wrote, "I would unite with anybody to do right and with nobody to do wrong."

After successfully escaping slavery and moving north to New York, Douglass officially won his freedom when British sympathizers paid off the slaveholder who still legally owned him. He was finally free to pursue the business of abolishing the American slave trade. Douglass joined various abolitionist organizations, read their weekly journals, and befriended leaders of the movement. In time, he was able to secure his own speaking engagements, and even began writing his first autobiography: *Narrative of the Life of Frederick Douglass, an American Slave*.

By the time of the Civil War, Douglass was one of the most famous black men in the country. After President Lincoln issued the Emancipation Proclamation, Douglass worked tirelessly to secure the equality that document promised.

Douglass served in several important political positions and was nominated vice president of the United States. At that point in U.S. history, no African American had ever gained such power.

An example and credit to all human beings, Frederick Douglass proved to the United States and the world that a person can rise to greatness even from the lowest circumstances.

In the year 1818. . .
- In the Treaty of 1818, the U.S. and Great Britain resolved issues following the War of 1812.
- *The Farmer's Almanac* was published for the first time in the United States.
- Chile officially gained independence from Spain.

Stand fast therefore in the liberty wherewith Christ hath made us free, and be not entangled again with the yoke of bondage.
GALATIANS 5:1 KJV

FANNY CROSBY

(1820–1915)
American Hymn Writer and Poet

The parents of baby Frances Jane Crosby, born March 24, 1820, became alarmed when they noticed their tiny infant's eyes were red and inflamed. A doctor wasn't readily available, so when Frances was six weeks old, her parents took her to a practitioner who was later exposed as a quack. After his prescribed treatment, the infection gradually healed, but the damage to little Frances's eyes was permanent. She was blind.

Fact: Fanny Crosby never earned more than four hundred dollars per year and gave away anything not needed for basic living.

Fourteen years later, Frances traveled by stagecoach to the New York Institute for the Blind. She described the day as the happiest of her life. Miss Crosby spent two decades at the institute. When her own schooling there was complete, she stayed on as a teacher. Nationally recognized as "The Blind Poetess," she was called upon many times to write and recite a poem for visiting U.S. presidents and other dignitaries.

In 1858, Frances (better known as Fanny) married a fellow teacher and blind musician, Alexander Van Alstyne, and they left the institute to begin a new life. Sadly, their only child died in infancy. Fanny's life work was redirected in 1864 when William Bradbury encouraged her to write Sunday school hymns.

Fanny Crosby perceived her blindness as a gift from God. She even believed the practitioner's mistake became a prelude to her writing nearly nine thousand hymns. "Blessed Assurance" and many other beloved hymns became favorites at D. L. Moody's revivals and are still being sung in congregations today.

In the year 1820. . .
- Pro-slavery and anti-slavery factions in the U.S. signed the Missouri Compromise.
- The Scottish Insurrection occurred in the United Kingdom.
- The Royal Astronomical Society was founded in London to promote astronomy.

I have learned the secret of being
content in any and every situation.
PHILIPPIANS 4:12

L'ABRI

Switzerland

God can use anything to draw people to Himself—even Swiss immigration laws. In the 1950s, an American couple named Francis and Edith Schaeffer were missionaries in Switzerland. But the Swiss government informed them that if they didn't buy property they'd be deported. So the Schaeffers bought a Swiss chalet.

The Schaeffers named their new home *L'Abri*, which is French for "the shelter." Their vision was to open their chalet to traveling students as a shelter from the secular pressures of the twentieth century. The students who took the Schaeffers up on their offer stayed anywhere from a week to several months. Anyone with an interest in studying Christianity and its relevance to modern life was welcome, both Christians and non-Christians alike.

Fact: Francis Schaeffer and L'Abri were credited with inspiring Christian evangelicals to political activism in the 1970s and '80s, particularly in the ongoing legal debate over abortion.

By the 1970s, L'Abri became a combination retreat center, commune, and seminary. There were no fixed courses or lectures. Students spent half of their days in individualized study, reading books and listening to recorded lectures based on their interests. The rest of their time was spent working around the property, cooking, cleaning, or doing maintenance work. Schaeffer wanted students to experience what it meant to live out what they believed in a Christian community.

What began as a place where students could openly discuss

their philosophical and religious beliefs grew into a worldwide academic evangelical organization. Although Francis Schaeffer died in 1984, L'Abri currently has residential study centers in the United States, Canada, South Korea, England, the Netherlands, and Sweden—in addition to its original location in Switzerland.

In the year 1955...
- The Warsaw Pact was signed by the USSR and other eastern European nations.
- Rosa Parks was arrested for refusing to give up her seat on a Montgomery bus.
- Marian Anderson debuted at the Metropolitan Opera in New York.

Be inventive in hospitality.
ROMANS 12:13 MSG

THE CRUSADES

Fight for the Holy Land

In the seventh century, Muslims took control of Jerusalem and ruled generously for more than four hundred years. They allowed large numbers of Christians to make pilgrimages to the holy places there. In the eleventh century, all that changed. The Seljuk Turks took over Jerusalem and visits no longer were allowed.

Fact: Like today's Muslim extremists, the Crusaders believed they were fighting a jihad or "holy war."

At the same time, Frenchman Urban II became pope and began to search for a strategy to repair a long-standing rift between the Eastern Orthodox Christians and the squabbling princes of the West. When Alexis of Constantinople asked for help fighting against the Muslim Turks, Urban instantly saw an opportunity to unite all Christendom by establishing a common enemy.

Urban played it up big, preaching loudly against "an accursed race utterly alienated from God" that had invaded Christian lands, and sending his representatives across Europe to recruit knights for the liberation of Palestine. Each crusader wore the Crusader's cross—a large red cross with four smaller crosses between the arms. As Crusaders made their way from Europe toward Jerusalem, they left a bloodbath of epic proportions in their wake. Assured by Urban that slaughtering infidels was a service to God with eternal benefits, they killed everything and everyone in their path.

In total there were seven crusades—all eventual failures. The Crusaders' conquest of the Holy Land was not permanent; they did not deter the advancement of Islam, nor did they heal the schism between East and West.

In the eleventh century. . .
- Viking king Canute ruled in England.
- The Great Schism separated the Roman Catholic Church from the Eastern Orthodox Church.
- Murasaki Shikibu wrote *The Tale of Genji,* considered by many to be the first novel.

*[Jesus said,] "To you who are listening I say: Love your enemies,
do good to those who hate you, bless those who curse you,
pray for those who mistreat you."*
LUKE 6:27–28

THE CHRISTIAN'S SECRET
OF A HAPPY LIFE

By Hannah Whitall Smith (1875)

For well over a century, *The Christian's Secret of a Happy Life* has opened the joy of Christianity to millions of believers worldwide. Its author, Hannah Whitall Smith, said that the idea for the book came as a response to someone who had noted the gloomy faces worn by most Christians. Smith set about to put a smile on those faces with a practical guide to all the things Christians have to be glad about.

Smith begins by differentiating God's part in the Christian life (to make us holy through the work of the Spirit) and our part (to trust God). She then deals with a series of challenges that beset Christians of all eras, such as doubts, temptations, and failure. She illuminates the joy that comes to the Christian who obediently follows God's will and experiences union with God. Smith's views on suffering reflect her belief that God does not cause, but uses trials, to strengthen the soul, elevate faith, and deepen understanding.

Fact: Hannah Whitall Smith wrote, "The God who is behind His promises and is infinitely greater than His promises, can never fail us in any emergency."

Throughout the book, Smith offers real-life examples to show how the Spirit of God works in the lives of believers. She repeatedly drives home the observable marks present in a Christian's attitude and actions that witness to an unbelieving world the transforming power of the Spirit.

The Christian's Secret of a Happy Life holds particular insight for today's Christians who live in a culture focused on human reason and emotions. Smith reminds readers that human feelings are notoriously changeable, whereas God's love remains eternally the same. For Christians then and now, that's something to smile about.

In the year 1875...
• Seventeen nations signed the Metre Convention, which created organizations to control metric standards.
• The Bombay Stock Exchange was founded.
• Matthew Webb swam the English Channel—the first person to do so.

*I praise you because I am fearfully and wonderfully made;
your works are wonderful, I know that full well.*
PSALM 139:14

THE DOXOLOGIES

"Gloria Patri" (1851) and "Praise God
from Whom All Blessings Flow" (1674)

A *doxology* is simply a short hymn of praise to God, used regularly in worship services. A number of doxologies are known, but two are most often used in churches.

The first—known as the "*Gloria Patri*"—is used by Catholic, Orthodox, and many Protestant churches. Considered both a hymn of praise and a short declaration of faith, it is said to be based on Ephesians 3:21 and Isaiah 45:17 in the King James Bible. The musical arrangement most often used with the "Gloria Patri" was composed by Henry Wellington Greatorex in 1851.

Fact: The apostle Paul used doxologies—addressed to God the Father, to Him through the Son, or with the Holy Spirit—in verses like Romans 11:36, Jude 25, and Ephesians 3:21.

> *Glory be to the Father, and to the Son,*
> *And to the Holy Ghost;*
> *As it was in the beginning, is now, and ever shall be,*
> *World without end. Amen, amen.*

The second doxology—widely used in English in Protestant churches—was originally the seventh and final stanza of the hymn entitled "Awake My Soul, and with the Sun." Thomas Ken, a bold, outspoken, seventeenth-century Anglican bishop, was the author of this evening worship hymn sung to the tune of "Old Hundredth." This was a sixteenth-century melody attributed to the French composer Loys Bourgeois and best known by the hymn "All People That on Earth Do Dwell" by William Kethe. It is credited with being the most famous of all Christian hymn tunes.

> *Praise God, from Whom all blessings flow;*
> *Praise Him, all creatures here below;*
> *Praise Him above, ye heavenly host;*
> *Praise Father, Son, and Holy Ghost. Amen.*

In the year 1851...
- The Taiping Rebellion began.
- California's Yosemite Valley was discovered.
- Western Union was founded.

> *You will be blessed when you come*
> *in and blessed when you go out.*
> DEUTERONOMY 28:6

CHRISTIAN RADIO BROADCASTING

Westinghouse started the first radio station in Pittsburgh, Pennsylvania, in 1920, using the call letters KDKA. The company's radio sets were becoming popular, and the station needed programming to keep the trend alive. As the station scrambled for program ideas to fill the airways, someone suggested the broadcast of a church service to test the feasibility of broadcasting from a remote location. One of the engineers belonged to Calvary Episcopal Church in Pittsburgh, so arrangements were made for the first Sunday evening in 1921. It was a hit and the program became a regular.

In the Chicago area, preacher Paul Rader was broadcasting his radio show from a rooftop, using a single telephone microphone. When he noticed that Chicago's WBBM was off the air on Sundays, he asked to use the studio. For fourteen hours each Sunday, he filled the airways with the sounds of preaching and a brass quartet. Using special, Sunday-only call letters, WJBT became the station "Where Jesus Blesses Thousands." By 1928 there were sixty religious radio stations. New rules by the Federal Radio Commission reduced that number to thirty, but those that survived were strengthened.

Fact: Some evangelical Christians opposed the introduction of Christian radio broadcasts, arguing that the Bible calls Satan the "prince of the power of the air" (Ephesians 2:2 KJV).

Most Christians saw Christian radio as far more than godly entertainment. It was viewed as a tool in their quest to disseminate the gospel to as many people as possible by whatever means possible. Donald Grey Barnhouse was the first to buy time on a national radio network, which made him in essence the first radio preacher. The first missionary radio station, HCJB, established in Quito, Ecuador, in 1930, was also the first radio station in the entire country.

In the year 1921. . .
• The Irish War of Independence ended.
• Warren G. Harding became the twenty-ninth president of the United States.
• Insulin was discovered by Canadian scientists.

What you say can mean life or death.
Those who speak with care will be rewarded.
PROVERBS 18:21 NCV

KEITH GREEN

(1953–1982)
Gospel Singer, Songwriter, and Musician

Controversial, sold-out, talented, blunt gospel singer Keith Green absolutely refused to accept the spiritual status quo. His sermons set to music plowed a new course for what Christian music could be.

As a teenager, Keith was restless. He was raised Jewish but had read the New Testament. The odd combination left him spiritually seeking. At fifteen, he ran away from home, looking for spiritual fulfillment and musical adventure. He experimented with drugs, Eastern mysticism, and free love. When he was nineteen, he met a girl named Melody. Together they started exploring matters of faith. At age twenty, Keith and Melody were married.

By the end of 1972, they had explored everything but the Bible and Christian Science. Keith didn't like the organized machine of Christian Science and so decided to deal with Jesus directly. Through simple prayers, he opened himself up to Christ, and Christ revealed Himself to Keith in a deep and profound way. Keith Green had found what he was looking for.

Fact: Keith Green said, "I repent. . .if my music, and more importantly, my life have not provoked you into godly jealousy or to sell out more completely to Jesus!"

After his conversion, Keith and Melody began to open their home to drug addicts and rejects. Talk of Jesus flowed freely. His music took a radical turn, too, and he began to pen such Christian classics as "You Put This Love in My Heart," "Oh Lord, You're Beautiful," and "You Are the One."

Although Keith Green's fame grew, his heart always remained for the lost. In 1982, his life (along with the lives of two of his children) was cut short by a tragic plane crash. His work, music, and ministry still continue on through the work of Last Days Ministries.

In the year 1953. . .
• Egypt, under Gamal Abdel Nasser, became a republic.
• The coronation ceremony took place for Queen Elizabeth II.
• Jonas Salk introduced his vaccine for polio.

Therefore, with minds that are alert and fully sober,
set your hope on the grace to be brought to you
when Jesus Christ is revealed at his coming.
1 PETER 1:13

ANGELINA AND SARAH GRIMKÉ

(1805–1879) / (1792–1873)
Abolitionists and Feminists

Flouting mid-nineteenth-century Southern sensibilities, sisters Angelina and Sarah Grimké argued for the abolition of slavery. As the daughters of a South Carolina judge and plantation owner, they had seen slaves suffer under the crack of the whip and witnessed the injustices and degradation slavery produces. The sisters' outspokenness made them unwelcome among their slave-holding neighbors, and they moved north, where they joined the Religious Society of Friends—the Quakers.

Sarah and Angelina were among the first women in the United States to lecture publicly against the institution of slavery in the South and racial discrimination in the North. Both wrote antislavery pamphlets that were burned in the South. Both received official warnings of arrest should they ever return home. Meanwhile, a number of religious leaders gasped at the spectacle of women voicing their opinion on political issues.

Fact: Sarah Grimké's writing presaged the modern feminist movement. Comparing the status of women to that of slaves, she demanded: "All I ask of our brethren is that they will take their feet from off our necks."

Noting that their negative comments on slavery highlighted the blatant sexism in American society, the sisters added to their campaign the issue of women's equality. While some abolitionists fought to keep the movement strictly focused on the plight of slaves, others, like the Grimkés, insisted on equality for both blacks and women.

Angelina married fellow abolitionist and feminist Theodore

Weld and settled with him in New Jersey. With Sarah, she opened a school, followed by another in New York. During the years of the Civil War, Angelina actively supported Abraham Lincoln in her writings and lectures. She continued to work to end racial discrimination and for women's suffrage until her death in 1879.

In the year 1879. . .
• The Zulu War ended with the Battle of Ulundi.
• Germany and Austria-Hungary formed the Dual Alliance.
• Gilbert and Sullivan's *The Pirates of Penzance* was first performed in New York.

We were all baptized by one Spirit so as to form one body—
whether Jews or Gentiles, slave or free—
and we were all given the one Spirit to drink.
1 CORINTHIANS 12:13

32

MAMERTINE PRISON

Rome

The Romans were a surly lot. Mess with them and you were apt to end up in a disgusting, damp, smelly prison—indefinitely. Offenders weren't sentenced to prison to pay for their crimes; they were thrown in prison until their *real* sentences could be carried out. It is believed that both Peter and Paul were held in Mamertine Prison in Rome prior to their executions.

Fact: The cross on the altar in the lower chapel is upside down in honor of the apostle Peter, whom tradition says was crucified upside down.

Located on the east side of the Capitoline Hill, Mamertine Prison is adjacent to the Roman Forum beneath the Chapel of the Crucifix. Constructed in the seventh century BC, originally the prison was a vast network of dungeons under the city's main sewer. By the time Peter and Paul spent their days underground, the prison consisted only of a small building with two cells, one on top of the other. These cramped, miserable spaces must have been particularly cold, damp, and drafty due to their proximity to the sewers. No wonder Paul asked Timothy to "come to me quickly. . .[and] bring the cloak that I left. . .at Troas" (2 Timothy 4:9, 13 NIV). He must have been wet and chilled to the bone.

The lower room, where the condemned were thrown, is round and made of pepperino and mortar. Today, a plaque hangs on the wall of the upper chamber, listing the names of some of the more famous prisoners, martyrs, and their persecutors. To one side is a red marble altar, and to the left of that stands a column said to be the one to which Peter and Paul were tied when they converted their guards to Christianity.

In the seventh century. . .
• The Scythians arrived in Asia.
• Tullus Hostilius became king of Rome.
• Nebuchadnezzar built the Hanging Gardens of Babylon.

*[Paul wrote,] This is my gospel, for which
I am suffering even to the point of being chained
like a criminal. But God's word is not chained.*
2 TIMOTHY 2:8–9

33

FIRE RAVAGES ROME

The infamous emperor Nero—great-grandson of Caesar Augustus—took control of the empire when he was just sixteen years of age. Perverted by power and ambition, he is alleged to have killed his mother, even though she married and possibly murdered his predecessor in order to gain him the empire. One of his grand schemes was to tear down about a third of Rome in order to build a series of palaces to be called the Neropolis. The Senate objected, but Nero got a lucky break.

In AD 64, a fire broke out in the shops and tenements surrounding Rome's mammoth chariot stadium—the Circus Maximus. The flames raged for ten days, leveling two-thirds of the city. Fires in the tenement areas of Rome were common, but this one was different. It was reported that Nero had the fire set intentionally and then sent thugs to keep citizens from fighting the fire. True or false, the result was the same—Nero got what he wanted. When the city was rebuilt at public expense, he seized the land needed to build his palaces.

Fact: Various reports have Nero fiddling while Rome burned, visiting a seaside resort, or running through the streets urging his soldiers to control the flames. Perhaps there's truth in all three.

Hoping to quell the rumors, Nero looked for a scapegoat and found one. He blamed the fire on an obscure Jewish sect called the Christians. Authorities rounded them up; some were crucified, others fed to wild animals at the Colosseum games, others used as human torches. Similar persecution, though sporadic, lasted for two and a half centuries. Interestingly, this persecution is thought to have been the greatest impetus for the growth of the early Church.

In the year 64. . .
- Phoenician writer Philo Byblos was born.
- Kushan forces defeated the Parthians to control Gandhara.
- Seneca the Younger wrote his *Letters to Lucilius* on moral issues.

Consider it pure joy, my brothers and sisters, whenever you face trials of many kinds, because you know that the testing of your faith produces perseverance. Let perseverance finish its work so that you may be mature and complete, not lacking anything.
JAMES 1:2–4

34

CONFESSIONS AND CITY OF GOD

By Augustine of Hippo (397, 413)

The tell-all exposé dates back not to the first sizzling disclosure heard on tabloid television, but to St. Augustine's *Confessions*, written in 397.

In his autobiography, Augustine grapples with some of the most intimate questions of spiritual life. He writes passionately and piercingly about his battle with temptations of the flesh as he struggled to live a holy life. *Confessions* covers Augustine's first thirty-five years, describing in detail his myriad sins and shortcomings, his youthful rebellion against God, and his ultimate acceptance of Christ.

Unlike a typical self-portrait, Augustine's *Confessions* hardly mentions—even omits—significant life events not connected to his spiritual growth, yet explores in detail minor events that pertain to his commitment to Christianity. With keen insight, he unflinchingly delves into the psychology of the human spirit. The authenticity of Augustine's voice and his willingness to bare his soul for the sake of guiding fellow spiritual travelers has endeared *Confessions* to generations of Christians.

Fact: St. Augustine wrote, "The mind gives an order to the body and is at once obeyed, but when it gives an order to itself, it is resisted. What causes it?"

Another of the prolific writer's classics is *City of God*, a history from a distinctly Christian perspective. Written after the Goths sacked Rome in 410, *City of God* defends Christians against the charge they were responsible for the disaster. Critics maintained that Christians, in worshipping the God of the Bible, had offended traditional Roman gods. Augustine points to the many and various calamities woven throughout Rome's long history. He then proceeds to explain these and contemporary events in light of the struggle between two societies, symbolized by Jerusalem, the City of God, and Babylon, the city of those in rebellion against God.

In the year 397. . .
- Saint Sulpicus Severus worked on his biography for Saint Martin of Tours.
- *Casa Candide* was founded following the death of Scottish monk Ninian.
- The Council at Carthage took place to discuss issues of canonization.

> *I do not understand what I do. For what I*
> *want to do I do not do, but what I hate I do.*
> ROMANS 7:15

35

"HIS EYE IS ON THE SPARROW"

Words by Civilla D. Martin (1905)
Music by Charles Gabriel (1905)

While staying in New York in the spring of 1905, Civilla Martin and her husband met and became good friends with a Christian couple, the Dolittles. Mr. Dolittle was crippled and used a wheelchair to get him to and from his business, and Mrs. Dolittle had been ill and bedridden for almost twenty years. During one of their visits with the couple, Civilla's husband commented on the couple's obvious optimism and happiness despite physical circumstances.

Mrs. Dolittle quickly responded, "His eye is on the sparrow, and I know He watches me." Her expression inspired Civilla Martin to verse the hymn that is still so popular today.

Fact: Ethel Waters sang "His Eye Is on the Sparrow" annually during Billy Graham crusades, making it one of the hallmarks of the events.

Many associate the song with the African American blues singer and actress Ethel Waters, who so loved this song that she used its title for her autobiography. In 1957, she sang this song as a solo while attending a Billy Graham crusade in Madison Square Garden. She says the experience changed her life forever.

Why should I feel discouraged, why should the shadows come,
Why should my heart be lonely, and long for heaven and home,
When Jesus is my portion? My constant friend is He:
His eye is on the sparrow, and I know He watches me;
His eye is on the sparrow, and I know He watches me.

Refrain:
I sing because I'm happy,
I sing because I'm free,
For His eye is on the sparrow,
And I know He watches me.

In the year 1905. . .
- Albert Einstein published his theory of special relativity.
- Women were granted suffrage in Queensland, Australia.
- The Brooklyn Public Library banned Mark Twain's *The Adventures of Huckleberry Finn.*

[Jesus said,] "Are not two sparrows sold for a penny? Yet not one of them will fall to the ground outside your Father's care. And even the very hairs of your head are all numbered. So don't be afraid; you are worth more than many sparrows."
MATTHEW 10:29–31

36

DAVEY AND GOLIATH

American Television

What in claymation is this? Gumby and Pokey, move over and make room for Davey and Goliath. The animated clay figures developed by Gumby creators Art and Gloria Clokey stepped into American living rooms in 1960.

Now a classic television series, *Davey and Goliath* began as fifteen-minute episodes designed to teach Christian values to children. Faith-based stories featured small-town kid Davey Hansen and his talking dog, Goliath. Goliath, whose voice remains unheard by anyone but Davey and the audience, acted as Davey's faithful conscience. Action and dialogue expanded on issues of character, responsibility, and faith in God in an imaginative and entertaining way. *Davey and Goliath* was ahead of its time in children's programming by delving into substantive topics of race relations and near-death experiences. The original small cast of Davey, his dog, and family members expanded to an assembly of more than twenty assorted claymations.

Fact: Davey and Goliath has become a pop-culture icon for nostalgic baby boomers. Licensed Davey products—from bobbleheads to T-shirts—remain popular items.

The Lutheran Church in America (now ELCA) produced the award-winning American television program and its numerous specials. For twenty years, *Davey and Goliath* drew fans throughout the United States and abroad. Several cable stations across the country still air episodes.

While dear to the hearts of baby boomers who grew up with the Saturday morning show, *Davey and Goliath* is attracting new fans among today's young people. Davey and friends have appeared at recent ELCA church gatherings, and the characters are featured in church materials for vacation Bible school. In 2003, a one-hour documentary, *Oh Davey! History of the Davey and Goliath Television Series*, was broadcast on network television across the United States and Canada.

In the year 1960. . .
• The Mau Mau Uprising ended in Kenya.
• Richard Nixon and John F. Kennedy held the first televised presidential election debate.
• The farthing was no longer considered legal tender in the United Kingdom.

"Reject the wrong and choose the right."
ISAIAH 7:15

37

GEORGE FRIDERIC HANDEL

(1685–1759)
Composer of *Messiah*

Although Handel's *Messiah* is considered one of the greatest compositions of all time and revered as the pinnacle of worship music, Handel, the man, was often at great odds with the church of his day. His first English oratorio, *Esther*, was met with derision by the church. They found it vulgar that the words of God would be spoken in a theater. One minister even claimed it was the work and will of Satan. The bishop of London banned the work from being performed. Handel defied the church and performed it instead for the royal family, who loved it.

Handel's next religious work, *Israel in Egypt*, was met with similar disdain. Christians went so far as to tear down playbills posted in the streets. All of this angered the devout Handel, who often became irritated by his contemporaries.

Handel was hopeful that his next work, *Messiah*, would fare better. His wealthy friend Charles Jennens commissioned him to write the music to a libretto about the life of Christ and His redemptive work for mankind. Though depressed, Handel decided to accept the work. In twenty-four days, Handel had composed 260 pages.

Fact: J. S. Bach is reported to have said, "[Handel] is the only person I would wish to see before I die, and the only person I would wish to be, were I not Bach."

On its premiere in London, the name was changed to *A New Sacred Oratorio* to quell cries of blasphemy over its original title, *Messiah*. The king arrived and was so moved by the opening refrains of the "Hallelujah Chorus" that he stood upon hearing it. Handel produced the work thirty times before his death on the day before Easter in 1759.

In the year 1685. . .
- James Scott, Duke of Monmouth, asserted his right to reign in the Monmouth Rebellion.
- Louis XIV of France revoked the Edict of Nantes, allowing the persecution of Protestants.
- French explorers founded Fort Saint Louis in present-day Texas.

For to us a child is born, to us a son is given, and the government will be on his shoulders. And he will be called Wonderful Counselor, Mighty God, Everlasting Father, Prince of Peace.
ISAIAH 9:6

FRANCES RIDLEY HAVERGAL

(1836–1879)

Poet, Songwriter, and Philanthropist

The inner life of the spirit captivated Frances Ridley Havergal. As a child, she wrote poems of remarkable depth and fluidity and was published in several highly regarded religious periodicals. Her philanthropic work began when, as a schoolgirl, she formed the Flannel Petticoat Society to provide clothing for children of poor families. While her life's mission consisted of telling others about Christ and encouraging faithfulness to Him, she actively tended to temporal matters as well.

Havergal's own life was marked by a series of heartbreaking losses. When Havergal was eleven, her beloved mother passed away. Havergal later recounted her anguish as she watched her mother's funeral procession leave the family home and turn in the direction of the churchyard. When she came of age, the man with whom she fell in love did not share her faith.

Fact: Frances Ridley Havergal wrote of her musical inspiration: "I believe my King suggests a thought, and whispers me a musical line or two, and then I look up and thank Him delightedly and go on with it."

Rather than marry an unbeliever, she chose to remain unmarried. Throughout her life, Havergal endured long periods of ill health.

Troubles and trials neither weakened her faith nor dampened her spirit. Rather, she accepted personal hardship as necessary to enable her to encourage others, for in suffering she found strength and solace in God's Word. Two of her best-known hymns—"Take

My Life and Let It Be" and "I Gave My Life for Thee"—express truths known only to those who have traveled through shadows and darkness by the light of faith in Christ.

Havergal died at age forty-three. Her last utterance, "I *did* so want to glorify Him," seems to have been richly fulfilled.

In the year 1836. . .
• The Battle of the Alamo ended.
• Charles Darwin returned to Britain after his voyage on the *Beagle*.
• János Irinyi invented a noise-free phosphorous match.

Grace to all who love our Lord Jesus Christ
with an undying love.
EPHESIANS 6:24

MARS HILL

Athens, Greece

On a rocky plateau, midway between Athens' Acropolis and the ancient Agora, lays Mars Hill. The Romans named this limestone outcropping after their god of war, Mars. The Greeks, who called the god of war Ares, called the site Areopagus, the Hill of Ares. But many simply referred to this site as the "Hill of Curses." That's because this arena-like setting was where the Murder Tribunal of Athens met to try those accused of some of the city's most heinous crimes.

Fact: In the fourth century, a pagan temple was dedicated to the mythological goddesses of vengeance at the foot of Mars Hill. Murderers could find sanctuary there.

When the apostle Paul visited Mars Hill, the summit was filled with philosophers, not magistrates—and it was Paul who put their gods on trial. If Paul arrived in Athens via the port of Piraeus, which would have been a logical point for him to enter the city, he would have passed temple after pagan temple on his way to the city center. An ancient proverb stated that Athens had "more gods than men." After passing statues of Poseidon, Athena, Zeus, Apollo, and Hermes on his way into town, Paul may have been inclined to agree.

But it was the altar "to an unknown god" that Paul brought to the attention of the Stoic and Epicurean philosophers who spent their days debating the latest ideas. Using this altar as a sermon illustration, Paul introduced the one true God into the philosophers' debates. Paul's words on Mars Hill marked a shift in how he spread the gospel. This time he preached to strangers, instead of being invited to speak by friends.

In the fourth century. . .
• Christianity became the official religion of the Roman Empire.
• The Huns entered Europe.
• The Battle of Fei River was fought in China.

Paul then stood up in the meeting of the Areopagus and said: "People of Athens! I see that in every way you are very religious. . . . I even found an altar with this inscription: TO AN UNKNOWN GOD. So you are ignorant of the very thing you worship—and this is what I am going to proclaim to you."
ACTS 17:22–23

40

THE FIRST MODERN TRANSLATION
OF THE ENGLISH BIBLE

The man of dictionary fame took upon himself the formidable task of producing an American English translation of the Bible.

Noah Webster worked from the King James Version (KJV), which he revered for its accuracy and expressiveness. He planned to make no changes except where necessary: to replace obsolete words and words that had changed meaning over the previous two centuries; to update old spellings and exchange Britishisms for American idioms; and to substitute certain descriptive, but earthy, terms sprinkled throughout the King James Version with more gently stated euphemisms compatible with American sensibilities. In tone and format, however, Webster closely followed the KJV. So closely, in fact, that critics cited many areas where he could have made significant changes to promote American English usage. Nonetheless, Webster's accurate and readable translation retains its place as the first modern translation of the English Bible.

Fact: Noah Webster wrote, "In my view, the Christian religion is the most important and one of the first things in which all children under a free government ought to be instructed."

Published in 1833, Webster's Bible offers lexicographers today a base for comparing nineteenth-century American English with the English of the King James Bible. His work influenced American translators who followed him fifty years later with the American Standard Version, the source of the Revised Standard Version of 1952.

While Webster's Bible never achieved great acceptance among the Bible-reading public of his day, it's realizing some degree of popularity now. Webster's translation ranks among the few modern English texts that, because of age, is in the public domain. Writers can quote the Bible without seeking permission from, or paying royalty to, the publisher.

In the year 1833. . .
- The British Parliament began to free slaves in the British Empire with the Slavery Abolition Act.
- Britain claimed the Falkland Islands.
- The Leonid meteor shower was first sighted.

*Glory in his holy name; let the hearts
of those who seek the LORD rejoice.*
PSALM 105:3

41

THE CROSS AND THE SWITCHBLADE

By David Wilkerson (1962)

What happened on the streets of New York City's toughest neighborhoods held no personal interest for David Wilkerson, pastor of a rural church in Pennsylvania. One picture, however, changed his perspective.

The brutal murder of a polio victim by members of a New York street gang led to one of the most sensational trials in 1950s America. Seven boys stood accused of the crime, all members of a Coney Island gang. A *Life* magazine portrait of one of the boys—young, confused, angry—caught the pastor's attention. Wilkerson felt prompted by the Holy Spirit to help the boy, but he pulled back, having never been to the city before and without personal knowledge of gang culture.

The Lord prevailed, however, and Wilkerson went to New York. *The Cross and the Switchblade* tells what happened when he took the simple message of the gospel into the violent world of criminal gangs. Cowritten with Elizabeth and John Sherrill, the book describes Wilkerson's highly publicized but failed effort to visit the jailed gang members. The fiasco earned him the street credentials that won him the trust and acceptance of their friends still on the street.

Fact: *The Cross and the Switchblade*, now translated into thirty-five languages, has sold more than fifteen million copies and continues to inspire readers the world over.

Wilkerson resigned his ministry in Pennsylvania and went on to work with young drug addicts, alcoholics, gang members, and troubled teens who called the violent streets of New York's inner city their home. He established Teen Challenge, an outreach program and shelter, and has brought untold numbers of teenagers to Christ through his ministry.

In the year 1962. . .
• The Cuban Missile Crisis ended.
• Nelson Mandela was arrested and imprisoned.
• Snow fell in San Francisco for the first time in ten years.

[Jesus said,] "I was in prison
and you came to visit me."
MATTHEW 25:36

42

"HOLY, HOLY, HOLY"

Words by Reginald Heber (1826)
Music by John B. Dykes (1861)

Preacher, poet, hymnist, scholar—Reginald Heber wore a variety of hats and wore each one well. Born to a wealthy family in Cheshire, England, he distinguished himself as a gifted student. After completing his academic education and receiving his ordination, Heber was appointed rector at an Anglican parish in Shropshire, where he was admired and respected for his service, compassion, and generosity. Later, he lectured at Oxford, then served as missionary bishop of Calcutta (now Kolkata), India.

Heber regularly wrote poems, sermons, and hymns. The hymns often pertained to a specific time of year in the liturgical calendar. "Holy, Holy, Holy," for example, was written for Trinity Sunday. He attempted to secure official authorization to use his hymns in the church, but the Bishop of London withheld permission. Heber saw a few hymns printed in the *Christian Observer*, but most of his work was published after his death under the title *Hymns Written and Adapted to the Weekly Church Service of the Year* (1827). His hymns became Christian favorites, including "From Greenland's Icy Mountains," "Brightest and Best of the Sons of the Morning," and "The Son of God Goes Forth to War."

Fact: Alfred Lord Tennyson called "Holy, Holy, Holy" one of the finest hymns ever written.

In 1861, John B. Dykes, a musician and composer, wrote the tune "Nicaea" for Heber's "Holy, Holy, Holy." Dykes chose the tune's name because Heber's text so clearly proclaims the Trinity, a doctrine articulated at the Council of Nicaea in 325.

Holy, holy, holy! Lord God Almighty!
Early in the morning our song shall rise to Thee;
Holy, holy, holy, merciful and mighty!
God in three Persons, blessed Trinity!

In the year 1826. . .
- Joseph Niépce took the first surviving photograph of buildings outside a window.
- Samuel Morey received a patent for his internal combustion engine.
- The American Temperance Society formed in Boston, Massachusetts.

"Holy, holy, holy is the Lord God Almighty,
who was, and is, and is to come."
REVELATION 4:8

43

THE FISH SYMBOL

Long before Christians affixed fish symbols to the bumpers of their cars, they were chiseling them into the rock walls of Rome's catacombs. The catacombs provided a relatively safe place for third-century Roman Christians to meet during periods of persecution, and the fish marked the spot. Brave believers also found a place near the doors of their homes to etch a fish symbol, thus letting other Christians know they were welcome. Presumably, the symbol provided bait for knowledgeable officials, too.

Fact: Early Christians, it's believed, used the fish symbol to identify each other. One would discreetly draw half the fish in the dirt; a fellow believer would complete the picture.

The fish symbol is a natural sign for Christianity. Many of Jesus' disciples made a living as fishermen, and fish and fishing are mentioned repeatedly in the four Gospels. There's also a Greek angle, Greek being the original language of the New Testament. The simple fish outline resembles the first letter of the Greek alphabet, alpha. In the book of Revelation, Jesus refers to Himself as the Alpha and Omega—something like the Greek *A* to *Zed*. The Greek word *IXqYΣ* (transliterated to "ichthus") means *fish*. The five Greek letters also form an acrostic, where each letter stands for a word: In English, the acrostic spells out "Jesus Christ God's Son Savior." Since most Christians today converse in keyboard rather than biblical Greek, the fish symbol has taken on a distinctly modern look: <><.

The fish marking cars, key chains, businesses, and personal stationery, has reeled in parody. The Darwin fish sprouts "evolved" legs with Darwin's name inside, continuing the debate of humankind's origins. Jumping out of the whole creationism-evolution net, the Trek fish sports the tail of the USS *Enterprise*.

May the fish be with you.

In the third century. . .
• The Roman Empire nearly fell in the Crisis of the Third Century.
• The Han Dynasty ended in China.
• The Baths of Caracalla were completed.

"Come, follow me," Jesus said,
"and I will send you out to fish for people."
MARK 1:17

DAVID LIVINGSTONE

(1813–1873)
Missionary to Central Africa

Though regaled as a national hero upon his death and buried in Westminster Abbey, missionary, explorer, and abolitionist David Livingstone was no example of Christian warmth and kindness. Within Africa, he didn't get along with other Westerners. He fought with other missionaries and explorers. White Afrikaners drove him out whenever he spoke out against intolerance. He even had problems with the London Missionary Society, who felt his explorations were a distraction to his mission work.

Whatever he did in Africa, however, David Livingstone always thought of himself first and foremost as a missionary. One of his primary objectives was to open a "Missionary Road," or "God's Highway" as he called it—a trail fifteen hundred miles into the interior to bring Christianity and civilization to the unreached peoples there. He wished to make the Zambezi River passable, so that Christian commerce could reach deep into the heart of the continent.

Fact: David Livingstone said, "Without Christ, not one step; with Him, anywhere!"

Livingstone went on to find the source of the Nile and was the first Westerner who saw Victoria Falls. Throughout it all, he stirred up public support through his books and letters for the abolition of slavery.

In 1871, *New York Herald* newspaper reporter Henry Morton Stanley found Livingstone in the town of Ujiji on the shores of Lake Tanganyika and greeted him with the now famous words,

"Dr. Livingstone, I presume?" Stanley urged Livingstone, now late in his life, to leave Africa, but Livingstone would not budge. He was determined to stay until his mission was complete.

In the year 1813. . .
• The term "Uncle Sam" was used in reference to the U.S.
• Jane Austen's novel *Pride and Prejudice* was published.
• Tecumseh and British forces led by General Procter led a siege on Fort Meigs.

Ye came near unto me every one of you, and said, We will send men before us, and they shall search us out the land, and bring us word again by what way we must go up, and into what cities we shall come.
DEUTERONOMY 1:22 KJV

JOAN OF ARC

(c. 1412–1431)
Martyr and Military Leader

Contrary to "funny Sunday school answers," Joan of Arc was *not* Noah's wife.

Jeanne la Pucelle, Joan the Maid, was born in Champagne, a region of northeastern France that had been embroiled in conflict between French loyalists and the English for more than one hundred years. Though an illiterate peasant girl, Joan exhibited piety and intelligence as a child. In her early teens, she discerned inner voices accompanied by a blaze of light that invited her to save France from the English.

Joan gained an audience with King Charles VII and convinced him of her God-sent purpose. An assembly of churchmen examined her and found her to be deeply devout and consecrated to God, adding credibility to her claims. The girl was provided with a suit of armor, and she joined a campaign against the English army besieging the town of Orléans. The French victory at Orléans led to further successes, but political intrigue, apathy, and deceit led to Joan's capture and imprisonment under English command.

Fact: More has been written about Joan of Arc than any other person of the Middle Ages—male or female.

The English, beaten in battle by the wisp of a girl, wanted to get rid of the source of their embarrassment in short order. A tribunal of politically motivated churchmen tried Joan for witchcraft, found her guilty, and sentenced her to die by fire in the marketplace of Rouen. Twenty years after her death, Pope

Callistus III held a second trial and Joan was cleared of all charges.

Historians credit Joan of Arc—both her military skills and her martyrdom—with uniting and invigorating the French to eventually drive the English from their country.

In the year 1431. . .
- The Council of Basel began.
- The MacDonalds defeated forces sent by James I at the Battle of Inverlochy.
- The University of Poitiers was founded in France.

Brethren, give diligence to make your calling and election sure: for if ye do these things, ye shall never fall.
2 PETER 1:10 KJV

THE METROPOLITAN TABERNACLE

London

Though the Metropolitan Tabernacle in London is a relatively new building, the heritage of the tabernacle holds a memorable place in history. It began with the Tabernacle Fellowship, a community of Baptists who braved persecution when the British parliament banned Christian organizations from meeting together in 1650. For thirty years, the fellowship secretly met in a widow's home. In 1688, shortly after the ban was lifted, the Tabernacle Fellowship built the New Park Street Church near London's Tower Bridge.

Fact: Spurgeon and his congregation chose their Metropolitan Tabernacle location because it was believed to be the site where clergy and laymen (the "Southwark Martyrs") were burned.

In the early 1800s, under the leadership of Dr. John Rippon, the New Park Street Church became the largest Baptist congregation in Great Britain. But it was twenty-year-old pastor Charles Haddon Spurgeon who really helped the church flourish. Within weeks of Spurgeon's arrival, the growing church needed a larger venue. Five years later, the Metropolitan Tabernacle was under construction. In the interim, the church met at the Royal Surrey Gardens Music Hall, which held up to ten thousand people.

Completed in 1861, the Metropolitan Tabernacle was the largest church building of its day, seating 6,500 congregants. Historians consider Spurgeon's Metropolitan Tabernacle the precursor to modern-day megachurches. But the church burned to the ground twice, once in 1891 and again during air raids in World War II. The impressive stone portico survived both fires. In 1957, the rest of the church was rebuilt within the perimeter of the original church building. Although few residents remained in central London after the war, by the 1970s the congregation of the Metropolitan Tabernacle began to flourish once more.

In the year 1861...
• Fort Sumter was attacked—the American Civil War began.
• Jefferson Davis became president of the Confederate States of America.
• An assassination attempt on Abraham Lincoln—known as the Baltimore Plot—failed.

> *"Keep watch over yourselves and all the flock of which the Holy Spirit has made you overseers."*
> ACTS 20:28

47

THE FUNDAMENTALS PUBLISHED

Say "fundamentalist," and most people picture a televangelist calling down a shower of fire and brimstone on a godless nation. The Protestant fundamentalist movement, however, began with noble intentions in the early years of the twentieth century.

A series of twelve polemical pamphlets called *The Fundamentals* were issued in 1910 by a coalition of conservative Protestants. The pamphlets articulated ninety articles of belief defined as fundamental to Christianity. In the same year, the General Assembly of the Northern Presbyterian Church published "the five fundamentals" of Christian doctrine, including the inerrancy of the Bible, the virgin birth of Christ, the authenticity of Christ's miracles, His sacrificial death, and His physical resurrection. Both *The Fundamentals* and "the five fundamentals" addressed specific points of doctrine conservative Protestant leaders believed were being challenged by science, liberalism, and modernism.

Debate on the subject flared across mainline denominations. Many churches split over issues raised by fundamentalists and congregants who espoused more liberal views. Those who stood by fundamentalist principles broke off from their parent denominations to set up new denominations or independent congregations.

Fact: Some authors of articles in *The Fundamentals* used early twentieth-century archaeological discoveries as proof of the Bible's authority as an accurate historical document.

Fundamentalist influence increased as conservative Protestants lobbied state legislators for conservative social causes. In the last several decades of the twentieth century, influential conservative talk-radio stations and television ministries multiplied, pulling in audiences of fundamentalists, evangelicals, and Pentecostals, among others. Today, fundamentalists write books, produce movies, and set up websites to reach even broader audiences. Though a movement highly critical of popular culture, fundamentalism continues to enthusiastically adopt and deftly use the world's newest technology.

In the year 1910. . .
• Earth passed through the tail of Halley's Comet.
• New York's Beaux-Arts-styled Penn Station opened.
• Women protested poor working conditions in the Chicago Garment Workers Strike.

Test them all; hold on to what is good.
1 THESSALONIANS 5:21

48

THE EAGLE AND CHILD PUB

Oxford, England

From 1939 until 1962, the Eagle and Child Pub was more than just a good place in Oxford, England, to grab a pint. It was home to meetings of the Inklings, a group of Christians who met in a private sitting room, now known as the Rabbit Room, at the rear of the establishment. The Inklings met weekly, every Monday or Friday, before lunch. Gathered on worn armchairs and settees in front of the small fireplace, the Christian scholars discussed literature, theology, and life.

Though nineteen men are known to have been a part of the Inklings at one time or another, two names stand out from the rest—C. S. Lewis and J. R. R. Tolkien. A decade before the Inklings was established, Tolkien was instrumental in Lewis's conversion to Christianity. Though Lewis's subsequent books of Christian apologetics, including *Mere Christianity*, earned him the reputation of being one of the most influential Christian writers of the twentieth century, it was Lewis's and Tolkien's works of fantasy that captured the widest audience. To date, Lewis's Chronicles of Narnia and Tolkien's Lord of the Rings trilogies have sold more than one hundred million and one hundred fifty million copies, respectively.

Fact: Though a plaque in the "Bird and Baby" commemorates the Rabbit Room as where the Inklings read drafts of their manuscripts, that actually took place in Lewis's room at the university.

In 1962, the Inklings switched their long-standing allegiance from the "Bird and Baby" (as the pub is nicknamed) to the Lamb and Flag Pub across the street. But visitors from around the world continue to visit the renowned Eagle and Child Pub to remember the gifted men of faith who once met within its walls.

In the year 1939. . .
• Germany invaded Poland.
• The World's Fair was held in New York.
• The classic film *The Wizard of Oz* opened.

> *[Jesus said,] "If there is no readiness, any trace of receptivity soon disappears. That's why I tell stories: to create readiness, to nudge the people toward receptive insight."*
> MATTHEW 13:13 MSG

"JESUS LOVES ME"

Words by Anna B. Warner and David Rutherford McGuire (1860) / Music by William B. Bradbury (1862)

This simple yet profound song first appeared in the novel *Say and Seal*, in a scene of a Sunday school teacher singing words of encouragement to a dying boy. The book's author, Susan Warner, asked her sister Anna—who regularly wrote hymns as part of a ministry to cadets at nearby West Point—to create a song for her story. Later, when Anna's simple poem was set to music by composer William B. Bradbury (who also wrote tunes for hymns such as "My Hope Is Built" and "He Leadeth Me"), "Jesus Loves Me" became a national and international favorite.

Fact: Recording artist Whitney Houston sang a version of this simple Sunday school song in her movie, *The Bodyguard*.

The second stanza of Anna Warner's original work is rarely found in hymnals—the lines refer to the dying boy of Susan's novel. Many modern hymnals include two additional stanzas written in 1971 by an Anglican priest, David McGuire. He based his contribution on the story of Jesus and the children in Matthew 19.

A story involving this sweet tune holds that when John F. Kennedy's World War II patrol torpedo boat (*PT-109*) was rammed and sank in the Solomon Islands in 1943, island natives rescued the crew. Faced with a daunting language barrier, the natives began to sing "Jesus Loves Me"—a song they had learned from missionaries—and the navy crew joined in enthusiastically.

Jesus loves me! This I know,
For the Bible tells me so.
Little ones to Him belong;
They are weak, but He is strong.

Refrain:
Yes, Jesus loves me!
Yes, Jesus loves me!
Yes, Jesus loves me!
The Bible tells me so.

In the year 1860. . .
• South Carolina secedes from the Union following the election of
  Abraham Lincoln.
• The Pony Express began delivering mail between Missouri and
  California.
• British and French troops burned the summer palace at Peking.

This is love: not that we loved God, but that he loved us
and sent his Son as an atoning sacrifice for our sins.
1 JOHN 4:10

50

JOHN 3:16 AT FOOTBALL GAMES

John 3:16 is commonly cited as "the Bible in a nutshell." Jesus spoke the words of God's action on behalf of humankind to Nicodemus when the temple leader visited Him in the dark of night. Rollen Stewart took these same words to one of the most well-lighted places in America—nationally televised football games.

It all began in 1980 with Stewart's conversion to Christianity. Already familiar to sports fans as the Rainbow Man who popped up in front of cameras wearing a colorful Afro wig, Stewart exchanged the wig for signs bearing Bible verses, such as John 3:16. Media-savvy, he positioned himself so he'd be seen by viewers as cameras followed team plays.

Stewart had no occupation other than appearing in front of television cameras. He traveled with his wife, who also held up signs, and both of them lived out of their car. Stewart and his signs showed up at football games, golf tournaments, World Series games, the summer and winter Olympics, political conventions, the Indy 500, World Cup soccer championships, and even the wedding of Princess Diana and Prince Charles. He drew a small cadre of fellow sign flashers, giving the desired impression that they were "everywhere."

Fact: A kidnapping charge stemmed from Stewart's taking a hotel maid hostage in his room. A standoff with police and a SWAT team ensued.

In the late eighties, television and stadium officials started making it harder to capture on-camera attention. Other adversities struck: Stewart's wife left him; a drunk driver totaled his car; his money dwindled. Broke and homeless, Stewart wandered the streets of Los Angeles. Convinced the end was near, he set off stink bombs in several locations to punctuate his point. He was later convicted on more serious charges and is now serving three life terms in prison.

In the year 1980. . .
• Mount St. Helens erupted in Washington.
• Members of the Gang of Four were put on trial in China.
• The U.S. Olympic hockey team defeated the Soviet Union.

> *[Jesus said,]* "*God so loved the world that he gave his one and only Son, that whoever believes in him shall not perish but have eternal life.*"
> JOHN 3:16

51

MARTIN LUTHER

(1483–1546)
Founder of the Protestant Reformation

As a child in Germany, Martin Luther believed he was watched by a great and just God, powerful enough to make lightning strike a boy for any small sin. Martin also believed that no matter how well he lived, in the eyes of God he was always sinful. He thought only the virgin Mary and the saints could pardon his sins.

Years later, this burden still waged against his soul. Luther tried desperately to gain God's favor at the monastery where he studied. He wanted to be accepted and loved by God, so he fasted, performed good works, flagellated himself, said prayers, and even went on a pilgrimage. He became gaunt and depressed. The more he tried to please God, the more he became aware of his own sinfulness.

Fact: In a castle of the supportive Frederick II, Elector of Saxony, Luther grew a beard and lived incognito for nearly eleven months, pretending to be a knight called Junker Jörg.

There, finally, at the monastery, Luther received his own Bible, bound in red leather. Nothing he had ever received in his life meant so much to him. As he studied and researched the Bible, he began to understand its central truth: justification by faith alone. Luther wrote and taught on this principle, angering the pope. The church said he risked excommunication unless he recanted his words. Luther would not recant, and in so doing, initiated the Protestant Reformation.

Through his life and work, Luther emphasized that a person is saved by God's merciful kindness through the work of Christ, not by any human effort. A Bible translator, he encouraged the common people to read the scriptures and discover for themselves the message of life-affirming faith within its pages. Today, nearly seventy million Christians claim to belong to Lutheran churches worldwide, and another 320 million Protestants trace their history back to Luther's reforming work.

In the year 1483. . .
• Leonardo da Vinci sketched the first design for a parachute.
• The Duke of Gloucester usurped the English throne as Richard III.
• The Sistine Chapel opened.

Because of his great love for us, God, who is rich in mercy, made us alive with Christ even when we were dead in transgressions—it is by grace you have been saved.
EPHESIANS 2:4–5

52

CATHERINE MARSHALL

(1914–1983)
Inspirational Bestselling Author and Novelist

The beginning of Catherine Marshall's writing career was not an easy one. When her first husband, Peter Marshall, chaplain for the U.S. Senate, died suddenly from a heart attack, Catherine was left to raise their nine-year-old son alone. Later, she felt compelled to write a biography of her beloved and highly respected husband that would include some of his prayers and sermons. Unknown to Catherine at the time, that first book launched a writing career that would span the next thirty-four years.

Fact: Catherine Marshall wrote, "No matter how late the hour, no matter how desperate the moment, we cannot despair; the joy and the riches [God] has promised stretch like a shining road into the future."

At age forty-four, Catherine's life took another turn when she married a man with three children. In order to establish a new home and life, she placed on hold the writing of a novel she'd been working on for more than a year. Catherine and her new husband, Leonard LeSourd, editor of *Guideposts* magazine for more than twenty-eight years, soon realized they made a great writing team. Catherine's writing and Leonard's editing developed into a wonderful working relationship that became an integral part of their lives. Together they created plots and ideas for novels and even coauthored a book entitled *My Personal Prayer Diary*.

Inspired by her mother's story and mission to teach poor children in the Appalachian Mountains, Catherine took nine years to write her first novel. Published in 1967, *Christy* was hailed as Catherine's greatest writing accomplishment and eventually became a popular television series.

Despite many personal trials, including the death of two grandchildren and her own physical challenges from debilitating emphysema, Catherine consistently inspired and motivated others to the same deep intimacy with Christ she cherished.

In the year 1914...
• World War I—"the war to end all wars"—began.
• The Panama Canal opened.
• Babe Ruth began playing for the Boston Red Sox.

> *The LORD is the stronghold of my life.*
> PSALM 27:1

MOUNT SINAI

Middle East

Before God caught Moses' attention with a burning bush, before Moses received the Ten Commandments, before Moses ever stepped on Mount Sinai's holy ground, this peak in Egypt was already known as the "Mountain of God." Though some biblical scholars believe the actual location of the biblical landmark to be Jabal al-Lawz in Saudi Arabia, tradition has long linked this mountain on the Sinai Peninsula to Moses.

Fact: In 1975, more than three thousand ancient manuscripts were accidentally discovered behind one of the walls of St. Catherine's monastery.

For the last one thousand years, pilgrims have made the journey across the inhospitable, volcanic landscape of the Sinai Peninsula to Jebel Musa (as Mount Sinai is known in Egypt). The 7,498-foot mountain is considered a sacred spot by Muslims, Jews, and Christians alike. In AD 330, Helena (the mother of Roman emperor Constantine) built a chapel at the foot of the peak where it was believed Moses saw the burning bush. In 530, the Byzantine emperor Justinian fortified the chapel against invaders and built the Church of the Transfiguration. It still survives as part of the monastic complex of St. Catherine's, which is believed to be the oldest monastery in continuous existence.

Behind the monastery, the 3,750 "steps of penitence" lead visitors up a steep ravine to the mountain's peak. On Mount Sinai's summit is a mosque and a Greek Orthodox chapel. The chapel was only erected in 1934, but it was built on the foundation of a sixteenth-century church. Though the chapel is closed to the public, tradition holds that it contains the rock from which the Ten Commandments were cut.

In the year 1934. . .
- Chinese communists evaded forces sent by Chiang Kai-shek in the Long March.
- The Dust Bowl continued to affect farmers across Texas, Oklahoma, and Kansas.
- Writer Rudyard Kipling shared the Gothenburg Prize for Poetry with William Butler Yeats.

The LORD descended to the top of Mount Sinai and
called Moses to the top of the mountain. So Moses went up.
EXODUS 19:20

THE GREAT AWAKENING

American Revival

The Great Awakening was not one continuous revival; rather, it was several revivals in a variety of locations that went so far as to influence changes in doctrine and social and political thought.

The First Great Awakening (1730–1740) was sparked when preachers like George Whitefield arrived from England, where revival was already underway. Around the same time, preacher Jonathan Edwards from Massachusetts was putting forth the theology of "total dependence" on the transformative emanations of the Holy Spirit. The revival, or renewal, as some prefer to call it, swept the American colonies, bringing people back to a greater intimacy with God.

One important result of this revival was its impact on the hearts and minds of the colonists. They became emboldened to believe that they were not at the mercy of the Church of England. Several decades later, they realized that they were also not compelled to honor the authority of the English monarchy. They could install their own means of governance.

Fact: Though the two had doctrinal differences, Charles Wesley so admired George Whitefield that he prepared a hymn especially for his funeral, entitled "Servant of God, Well Done."

A common vision of freedom emerged that gave rise to the Declaration of Independence.

The Second Great Awakening (1800–1830) did for the unchurched what the First Awakening had done for church members. It firmly established the concept of personal salvation through repentance and dependence on Christ.

The Third Great Awakening (1860–1900) was literally interrupted by the Civil War. It produced the Social Gospel Movement and worldwide missionary work.

The Fourth Great Awakening (1960–1970) gave rise to megachurches and parachurch organizations that emphasized the gifts of the Holy Spirit.

In the year 1730. . .
• Cherokee leaders met with King George II in England.
• An earthquake struck the city of Valparaiso, Chile.
• French pirate Olivier Levasseur died.

I will give you a new heart and put a new spirit in you;
I will remove from you your heart of stone and give you a heart
of flesh. And I will put my Spirit in you and move you to
follow my decrees and be careful to keep my laws.
EZEKIEL 36:26–27

IN HIS STEPS

By Charles M. Sheldon (1896)

The phrase "*What would Jesus do?*" has become an icon of pop culture, but its origins date back more than a century. Charles M. Sheldon, a Congregational minister, coined the phrase in a series of sermon stories prepared for his congregation in Topeka, Kansas. As a ploy to increase attendance at the Sunday evening services, Sheldon began reading one sermon story per week. These explored moral dilemmas concerning poverty, deprivation, and inequality encountered in everyday life. Each ended with a dramatic cliff-hanger. The strategy was a huge success. The crowds came pouring in, eager to hear the next installment.

Fact: Due to a technical error, the copyright for *In His Steps* was deemed defective and the book passed immediately into the public domain. It was then published by dozens of publishers.

While Sheldon was reading his stories to his parishioners, they were also being published as a serial in the *Chicago Advance*, a religious weekly newspaper. Sheldon later put the story into book form and entitled it *In His Steps*. The result was a compelling novel about a group of people from a Chicago church who agree to base all their actions and choices for one year on the question, "What would Jesus do?" They find they are unable to settle for easy choices, instead opting for difficult but spiritually rewarding projects in service to others. The message of this book is said to have been the inspiration for the advancement of the social gospel, as well as a catalyst for change in the lives of many thousands of believers.

Some recent reviewers have complained that the book is stuffy and poorly written. Whether their assessments are true or not, no one can dispute the popular success of *In His Steps*. An estimated thirty million copies have been sold in the century since its original release.

In the year 1896. . .
- Athens hosted the first modern Olympics.
- The shortest recorded war, the Anglo-Zanzibar War, ended within an hour of beginning.
- The U.S. Supreme Court ruled in favor of racial segregation in *Plessy v. Ferguson*.

Follow my example, as I follow the example of Christ.
1 CORINTHIANS 11:1

"IT IS WELL WITH MY SOUL"

Words by Horatio G. Spafford (1873)
Music by Philip P. Bliss (1876)

Horatio and Anna Spafford were still grieving the death of a son when the great Chicago fire destroyed almost everything they owned. Two years later, in 1873, Horatio felt his family needed a vacation and arranged a voyage to Europe for himself and his family, where they were looking forward to hearing Dwight L. Moody preach.

Delayed because of pending business, Horatio sent Anna and his four daughters ahead of him on the ship *Ville du Havre*. Halfway across the Atlantic, a sailing vessel rammed the ship during the night, cutting it in half. In the confusion, Mrs. Spafford watched in horror as her four daughters were swept to their deaths. In an odd twist of fate, a falling mast struck her unconscious—and a wave carried her body to a piece of floating wreckage, where she later regained consciousness. When she and other survivors reached Wales, she cabled two words to her husband: SAVED ALONE.

Fact: The music, written by Philip Bliss, was named after the ship on which Spafford's daughters died, *Ville du Havre*.

Filled with sorrow, Horatio set sail on the earliest ship to join his grieving wife. When the ship reached the spot where his daughters were lost at sea, he wrote with courage from the depths of his soul the words to one of the most beloved hymns of all time, "It Is Well with My Soul."

When peace, like a river, attendeth my way,
When sorrows like sea billows roll;
Whatever my lot, Thou has taught me to say,
It is well, it is well, with my soul.

Refrain:
It is well, with my soul,
It is well, with my soul,
It is well, it is well, with my soul.

In the year 1873. . .
- The Panic of 1873 caused economic depression throughout the U.S. until 1879.
- Levi Strauss and Jacob Davis produced the first pair of blue jeans.
- Prince Edward Island joined the Canadian Confederation.

Have mercy on me, my God, have mercy on me,
for in you I take refuge. I will take refuge in the
shadow of your wings until the disaster has passed.
PSALM 57:1

MITSUO FUCHIDA

(1902–1976)
Evangelist

I was getting ready for church that Sunday morning when. . ." the unthinkable happened. Shortly before 8:00 a.m. on December 7, 1941, the Japanese Air Force launched a surprise attack on American shores. Two waves of Japanese warplanes bombed American battleships and military installations at and around Pearl Harbor, Oahu, Hawaii. Less than two hours later, American forces were left with 21 ships sunk or damaged; 347 aircraft destroyed or damaged; 1,178 American military and civilians wounded; and 2,403 American deaths, including 54 civilians.

Japanese commander Mitsuo Fuchida led the first wave of attacks and stayed behind to observe the second wave, even though U.S. fire had compromised his plane. Fuchida's voice relayed the message, *"Tora! Tora! Tora!"* ("Tiger! Tiger! Tiger!") back to his aircraft carrier to report that the surprise attack had succeeded.

Fact: Fuchida, who died in 1976, desired to be remembered primarily for the change of heart he experienced upon his conversion to Christianity.

Then there was American POW Jacob DeShazer, captured by the Japanese in 1942 after a bombing raid near Tokyo. While in prison, DeShazer embraced Christianity. After being liberated, he wrote an essay, "I Was a Prisoner of the Japanese," in which he described his capture, conversion, and decision to forgive his captors. DeShazer's widely read testimony fell into the hands of Fuchida. Influenced by DeShazer's story, he bought a Bible and he, too, embraced the gospel message.

In 1950, Fuchida met DeShazer, who had returned to Japan as a Christian missionary. DeShazer encouraged Fuchida in his Christian walk. While DeShazer continued to establish churches throughout Japan, Fuchida took on the work of an evangelist, spreading the gospel in Japan and Asian communities in the United States.

In the year 1902. . .
• Lord Salisbury retired from his post as British Prime Minister.
• Britain, Germany, and Italy blockaded Venezuelan ports in the Venezuela Crisis.
• The bell tower of St. Mark's Basilica collapsed.

"If you forgive other people when they sin against you, your heavenly Father will also forgive you."
MATTHEW 6:14

58

JOHN MILTON

(1608–1674)
Author of Paradise Lost

Author John Milton, still considered one of the greatest masters of English prose, suffered some of the most debilitating personal setbacks to befall a man of such achievement.

At St. Paul's school, young John Milton fell behind his classmates and was considered "slow" in learning. At age seventeen, he was teased by his classmates at Christ's College at Cambridge and called "the Lady" because of his delicate features. Shortly after admission, he was expelled for clashes with his tutor. Despite some initial success as a writer, he was silenced by the death of his friend, fellow student Edward King, who drowned in the English sea. A year later, another close friend, Charles Diodati, died and the personal loss struck him deeply.

Fact: Helen Keller founded the John Milton Society for the Blind in 1928 to bring spiritual guidance and religious literature to deaf and blind persons.

One month after their marriage, Milton's young bride left him and returned to her parents. Though she came back to him three years later, she died giving birth to a son. Not long after this tragedy, Milton, only forty-three years old, became totally blind. Milton remarried, but his second wife also died during childbirth. Then, his life was in danger from a new king who hated his political views. Authorities issued a warrant for his arrest, so the writer went into hiding.

After all these events, Milton produced his masterpiece, *Paradise Lost*, and his follow-up five years later, *Paradise Regained*.

His subject was the fall of man from God's grace and God's work to restore man to his former place. His essays on Republicanism are also source materials for the Constitution of the United States of America.

In the year 1608. . .
• Samuel de Champlain founded Quebec City.
• Captain John Smith was nominated council president for the Jamestown colony.
• Hans Lippershey introduced the first telescope in the Netherlands.

Jesus stopped and said, "Call him." So they called to the blind man, "Cheer up! On your feet! He's calling you."
MARK 10:49

59

D. L. MOODY

(1837–1899)
American Evangelist and Publisher

An everyman with a common touch, Dwight L. Moody believed that God could and did use average people for His glory. A simple man himself, Moody was never encouraged to read the Bible as a child in Northfield, Massachusetts, and he only acquired a fifth-grade education. Moody, instead, took to business and declared his goal of amassing one hundred thousand dollars, a fortune by 1800s standards. At seventeen, Moody moved to Boston to work in his uncle's shoe store, where he proved himself to be a gifted salesman. It was also in Boston that he gave his heart to the Lord.

In 1856, Moody moved to Chicago to continue his sales career. Soon after arriving, Moody joined the Plymouth Congregational Church and began to invite the people he met while recruiting new customers for his business. Later he moved to the First Methodist Church, but the traditional church school did not seem compatible with most of Moody's converts. In response to this, he found an abandoned shanty and began his own Sunday school. When it was simply overflowing, he received permission from the mayor to move into a large hall over North Market.

Fact: Moody promoted cross-cultural evangelism using The Wordless Book, a teaching tool with red, black, white, and gold colors on it, representing various aspects of the gospel message.

Within a year's time, the average attendance at his Sunday school was six hundred fifty. Sixty volunteers from various churches served as teachers. Becoming famous all over America, newly elected President Lincoln visited and spoke at the school.

In 1886, Moody addressed the church about establishing a school for young evangelists and church leaders. The result was the Chicago Evangelization Society, renamed Moody Bible Institute after Moody's death.

In the year 1837. . .
• The city of Chicago was incorporated.
• Charles Dickens' *Oliver Twist* first appeared in serial form.
• A fire destroyed parts of the Winter Palace in St. Petersburg.

Jesus said, Make all the people recline (sit down). Now the ground
(a pasture) was covered with thick grass at the spot,
so the men threw themselves down, about 5,000 in number.
JOHN 6:10 AMP

60

CHRISTINA ROSSETTI

(1830–1894)
Writer and Poet

Christina Rossetti was born into an artistic and highly educated London household. Her father, the poet Gabriele Rossetti, taught at King's College, her brother became the famed painter Dante Gabriel, and all four children of the household were writers. Christina and her sisters followed in their mother's commitment to the Anglican Church.

The Oxford or Tractarian Movement influenced Rossetti's spiritual development. The popular nineteenth-century movement tried, among other things, to recreate Anglican traditions of the previous century and protect the church against modern reforms and government intervention. The movement revived an interest in medieval literature, architecture, and culture. Rossetti's religious poetry, often marked by a sense of melancholy and yearning for a lost past, reflects the romanticism of her time.

While Rossetti composed nonreligious poems, ballads, love lyrics, and songs for various journals, her best-known work, *Goblin Market and Other Poems*, takes up biblical themes in a fairy tale ostensibly for children. "Goblin Market," the title poem, tells the story of two sisters tempted to "come buy" luscious fruit. One sister does, while the other does not. The refraining sister saves her nibbling sibling in a noble act of self-sacrifice.

Fact: Christina Rossetti wrote, "Obedience is the fruit of faith."

Rossetti remained unmarried, having refused two gentlemen's proposals for religious reasons. Never in good health, in her later years she suffered from increasingly debilitating bouts of Graves' disease—a thyroid disorder. Though she continued to write poetry, prose, and devotions; study scriptures; and read religious classics, she rarely left the sanctuary of her home.

In the year 1830. . .
- In France, the July Revolution began.
- Joseph Smith formed what would become the Church of Jesus Christ of Latter Day Saints.
- Hector Berlioz's *Symphonie Fantastique* premiered in Paris.

> *[Jesus said,] "If you keep my commands, you will remain in my love, just as I have kept my Father's commands and remain in his love. I have told you this so that my joy may be in you and that your joy may be complete."*
> JOHN 15:10–11

61

NAZARETH

Israel

Nazareth was Jesus' childhood home. Today, it's home to numerous churches built to commemorate that fact. The two most famous churches are the Basilica of the Annunciation and the Church of St. Joseph. The two churches are linked by a Franciscan convent built on the original site of the town of Nazareth.

Archaeological ruins below the Church of St. Joseph date to the first century. They include a cave believed to be the original workshop of Joseph, which was also used as the family's home. Tooled niches in the rock walls were typical in homes during the Roman period to store food and water. One of these was converted during the Byzantine era into a mosaic-tiled baptismal pool. Several churches have been built and destroyed on this site. The current Church of St. Joseph was completed in 1914.

Fact: The Basilica of the Annunciation has a website where visitors from around the world are encouraged to light a candle via the Internet.

The Church of the Annunciation marks the traditionally held location of Mary's home and her visit from the angel, Gabriel. (However, the Greek Orthodox Church believes Mary spoke to Gabriel at a nearby well, which is marked by the Greek Orthodox Gabriel's Church.) The first shrine built on this spot was an altar constructed during the fourth century. Several churches were built after that, the fourth of which was destroyed in 1955 to construct the modern-day basilica. The largest Christian basilica in the Middle East, the church's interior is decorated with mosaics, banners, and a variety of art that has come from church communities worldwide.

In the year 1914. . .
• German forces occupied Brussels.
• The last American troops left Veracruz in the Mexican Revolution.
• *Dubliners* was published.

God sent the angel Gabriel to Nazareth,
a town in Galilee, to a virgin pledged to be married
to a man named Joseph, a descendant of David.
LUKE 1:26–27

62

GUTENBERG PRODUCES THE FIRST PRINTED BIBLE

Mainz, Germany

The age of mass communication opened when Johann Gutenberg's Latin Bibles rolled off the press. Or perhaps more accurately, were lifted off the press. Regarded as one of the most important inventions in history, the movable-type printing press made it possible to produce thousands of books in a short amount of time—a far cry from the laborious and time-consuming task of copying each individual page by hand.

Large books, such as the Bible, required some fifty thousand pieces of type. While printers already used wood or metal blocks to reproduce images, Gutenberg was the first to devise a way to move letters around and reuse them once a page had been copied the desired number of times. Gutenberg's metal blocks produced sharp and clear letters and images on rag cotton linen paper or vellum animal skin.

Published in Mainz, Germany, Gutenberg's Bible was bound in multiple volumes, each with three hundred pages. The text was printed in Latin—the prevailing language of the church, government, and scholarship. The majority of books to follow, however, including Bibles, were written in commonly spoken languages. Before Gutenberg's death in 1468, printers in cities throughout the continent and

Fact: The British Library's two copies of the Gutenberg Bible have been photographed digitally and made available online to everyone, not only scholars.

the British Isles had eagerly entered the profitable business of producing books, pamphlets, tracts, and posters.

Fewer than fifty original Gutenberg Bibles are known to exist today. Appraisers estimate that a complete Gutenberg would fetch more than thirty million dollars if offered for sale, making it one of the most valuable books in the world. Original Gutenberg Bibles, and sometimes individual pages, can be found in the collections of public institutions and private libraries.

In the fifteenth century. . .
• The House of York and the House of Lancaster fought in the Wars of the Roses.
• Turkish forces laid siege to Belgrade.
• The Byzantine Empire collapsed.

*I do not write to you because you do not know the truth,
but because you do know it.*
1 JOHN 2:21

63

KNOWING GOD

By J. I. Packer (1973)

First things first. Theologian and lecturer James Innell Packer's book, *Knowing God*, explores the Christian's primary goal in life: to strive for intimate knowledge of God. In clear and accessible language, Packer engages the reader with doctrinally sound and theologically focused chapters dealing with topics such as the Trinity, God's sovereignty, and God's will.

Fact: As a young man, Packer committed his life to Christian service and was ordained a priest in the Church of England, where he became an influential leader of the evangelical movement.

First written as essays to counter the trend toward easy answers to complex questions of faith, *Knowing God* quickly gained an enthusiastic following. The book clarifies for readers not versed in theology the meaning of terms heard in church but not readily understood.

Packer divides his book into three sections. In the first part, he calls Christians to personally commit themselves to study the character of God. Then, the book examines the attributes of God as revealed in the Bible. In its conclusion, *Knowing God* describes the happy consequences of a Christian's serious and continuing commitment to knowing God. Packer shows how the pursuit of God guides, comforts, and encourages believers through the changes and chances of life. Packer leads Christians to more fully realize the awesome attributes of God, the astonishing fact of being God's child, and the extraordinary joy of living life as a Christian.

Packard has penned other books and essays, yet he is best

known in Christian circles for the one title, *Knowing God*. Now considered a modern classic, the book was recognized in the year 2000 by the Evangelical Christian Publishing Association for achieving more than one million copies sold in North America.

In the year 1973. . .
- The Yom Kippur War began between combined Egyptian-Syrian forces and Israeli forces.
- The U.S. Supreme Court ruled on *Roe v. Wade*.
- The Sydney Opera House was completed.

> *Skilled living gets its start in the Fear-of-GOD,*
> *insight into life from knowing a Holy God.*
> PROVERBS 9:7 MSG

"JUST AS I AM"

Words by Charlotte Elliott (1835) /
Music by William B. Bradbury (1849)

Charlotte Elliott was born in Clapham, England, in 1789. When she was a young adult, she was a popular portrait artist and writer of humor. By age thirty, her health had declined, leaving her bedridden and despondent.

A turning point came in Charlotte's life in 1822 when Dr. Caesar Malan, a Swiss evangelist, visited the Elliott home and spoke these words to her, "You must come just as you are, a sinner, to the Lamb of God that taketh away the sins of the world." Dr. Malan's wise counsel concerning her spiritual and emotional state became her mission statement for life. Every year afterward, Miss Elliott celebrated that day as her spiritual birthday.

Fact: Charlotte Elliott wrote: "God sees, God guides, God guards me. His grace surrounds me, and His voice continually bids me to be happy and holy in His service just where I am."

Charlotte Elliott wrote "Just As I Am" in 1835—fourteen years after her life-changing experience. It was published that same year as only one of Miss Elliott's 115 hymns included in the second edition of *The Invalid's Hymn Book*. By writing the hymn from the voice of her own life's experience, she hoped to help raise funds for building a school for poor clergymen's children. That one hymn brought in more funds than all the other projects and bazaars combined.

Just as I am, without one plea,
But that Thy blood was shed for me,
And that Thou bidst me come to Thee,
O Lamb of God, I come, I come.

Just as I am, Thou wilt receive,
Wilt welcome pardon, cleanse, relieve;
Because Thy promise I believe,
O Lamb of God, I come, I come.

In the year 1835. . .
- The British Geological Survey is founded.
- King Leopold opened the first railway in continental Europe, the Brussels-Mechelen railway.
- P. T. Barnum began his career.

Then Jesus declared, "I am the bread of life. Whoever comes to me will never go hungry, and whoever believes in me will never be thirsty. . . . All those the Father gives me will come to me, and whoever comes to me I will never drive away."
JOHN 6:35, 37

PROMISE KEEPERS

W hat do you feel is the most important factor in changing a man spiritually, from immaturity to maturity?"

For the stereotypical macho American male, such a question might elicit little more than a dismissive grunt. But when football coach Bill McCartney asked fellow Christian Dave Wardell the same question, Wardell replied, "Discipleship."

Fact: Conferences, held in sports stadiums, are two-day, male-only events where speakers offer encouragement to participants to be godly husbands, fathers, brothers, and friends.

Wardell and McCartney founded Promise Keepers in 1990 around the concept of discipleship for men. They envisioned a nationwide revival of men who would take a stand for Jesus Christ, each man committing himself to seven promises: honor Jesus Christ; pursue meaningful relationships with other men; practice moral purity; build marriages on biblical values; support his local congregation with time and resources; strive for unity across racial and denominational lines; and make a positive difference in the world.

Liberal Protestant denominations generally do not support Promise Keepers' decidedly conservative evangelical brand of Christianity, and progressive women's organizations decry the all-male meetings and conferences. The latter fear the influence of Promise Keepers will work to reverse rights won by women in the last several decades.

Since its founding, Promise Keepers has attracted untold numbers of men through conferences, books, Bible-study resources, church outreach, the Internet, and radio broadcasts. Unlike most organizations, Promise Keepers does not keep a membership roster. Its gatherings, however, often attract hundreds of thousands of participants. Its 1997 rally, Stand in the Gap, on the National Mall in Washington DC, drew upward of seven hundred thousand men. Similar responses in other cities across the nation show the ideals of Promise Keepers continue to resonate with America's Christian men.

In the year 1990. . .
• East and West Germany reunified.
• Mary Robinson became the first female president in Ireland.
• The Leaning Tower of Pisa closed to the public.

"What God promised our ancestors he has fulfilled for us,
their children, by raising up Jesus."
ACTS 13:32–33

WATCHMAN NEE

(1903–1972)
Minister, Author, and Martyr

One of the most influential Chinese Christians ever, Watchman Nee was made famous by his book *The Normal Christian Life*. Based on talks he gave in Europe in the late 1930s, the work outlines his views on the book of Romans and describes what daily life should be for the Christian.

At the age of seventeen, Nee consecrated himself to Christ. He read as many as three thousand books to absorb and learn Christian doctrine and practice. From the early 1920s to the late 1940s, the Christian church flourished and grew in China, thanks in no small part to Nee's influence.

Fact: Watchman Nee wrote, "Our old history ends with the cross; our new history begins with the resurrection."

In 1952, Nee was arrested and imprisoned by Chinese authorities for his faith. His friends had advised him not to stay in China because of the persecution of Christians there, but Nee compared his homeland to a house on fire. He couldn't leave it. He had to stay and rescue as many as possible. During his incarceration, only his wife was allowed to visit him. Though he was forbidden to share about Christ in his letters, his final letter written on the day of his death, said, "In my sickness, I still remain joyful at heart." He remained in prison for twenty years.

His English name *Watchman* is a literal translation of his Chinese name. Pronounced "pinyin tùo," it means "Chinese knocker or plaque that sounded out to mark the hours of the night." Watchman Nee believed it was his duty to stay up through the dark of night to awaken men to the coming of Christ.

In the year 1903. . .
• Panama gained its independence from Columbia.
• The Wright brothers successfully flew the first airplane.
• The great French bicycle race, the Tour de France, began.

*I have been crucified with Christ; it is no longer I who live,
but Christ lives in me; and the life which I now live in the flesh I live
by faith in the Son of God, who loved me and gave Himself for me.*
GALATIANS 2:20 NKJV

MARY SLESSOR

(1848–1915)
Missionary

A human skull dangling from a pole greeted missionary Mary Slessor as she approached her new post. Old Town, a remote station in Calabara (now Nigeria), was not a hospitable place. The natives' reputation for cruelty and cannibalism kept most missionaries at a distance, but not Slessor. She went to teach the gospel of Jesus Christ.

Born in Scotland, Mary came from a working-class family. In her late twenties, she trained for mission work with the Presbyterian mission society and sailed for Calabar in West Africa.

Fact: Mary Slessor wrote, "I have always said that I have no idea how or why God has carried me over so many funny and hard places. . .except in answer to prayer made at home for me."

Once described as "a timid child," the now-intrepid woman entered a jungle of ferocious animals, poisonous insects, deadly diseases, and fearsome warriors. Her first assignment took her to Duke Town on the Calabar River.

Missionaries in Duke Town had established a chapel, school, and hospital. On any given Sunday, several hundred natives gathered at the mission station for services. Slessor taught at the mission school, learned the local languages, and traveled to neighboring villages. Despite the dangers, she ventured far inland, where tribes lived embroiled in terrifying superstitions and murderous customs. Slessor begged for permission to live among them. At last she received the coveted post: Old Town, deep in the jungle of Calabara.

Slessor's wisdom, love, and compassion for the people endeared her to the tribesmen, including the isolated and much-feared Okoyongs. Called "Ma Slessor," she was deeply respected among natives, traders, and missionaries alike. Recognized as an outstanding missionary, she was awarded the Silver Cross in Nigeria before her death in 1915.

In the year 1848. . .
• The United States Congress created the Oregon Territory.
• The Treaty of Guadalupe Hidalgo ended the Mexican-American War.
• Activists met at the Seneca Falls Convention to discuss women's rights.

> *[Jesus said,] "I have given you authority to trample on snakes and scorpions and to overcome all the power of the enemy; nothing will harm you."*
> LUKE 10:19

OBERAMMERGAU

Bavaria

In the early 1600s, much of what is modern-day Europe faced a seemingly unbeatable foe: the Black Death. As the bubonic plague swept the countryside, one small town in Bavaria boldly called on the only one they knew who could stop this indiscriminate executioner. They called out to God.

In 1633, nearly every family in Oberammergau had lost someone to the plague. So its citizens joined together and vowed that if God would spare their town, they would honor Him by performing a "Play of the Suffering, Death, and Resurrection of Our Lord Jesus Christ" every ten years until the end of time. As the number of deaths radically diminished, plans for the Passion play began to take shape. In 1634, on a stage erected on the still-fresh graves of the town cemetery, Oberammergau performed its first Passion play. Every decade for the last three centuries (except in 1870 and 1940 during times of war) has seen the Passion play grow in scope and popularity.

Fact: Every ten years, on the Ash Wednesday a year before the Passion play begins, the "Hair Decree" goes into effect: All the Oberammergau men in the performance stop cutting their head and facial hair.

The now world-famous Passion play is performed in years that end in a zero.

The pageant involves over two thousand actors, whose good moral standing is as crucial as their acting talent. Hundreds of musicians and stage technicians also take part in the production. Anyone involved in the musical extravaganza must have lived in

Oberammergau for at least twenty years. Performed in an open-air theater before an audience of more than five thousand, the play lasts more than six hours and is repeated five days a week from May through September.

In the year 1634...
• Polish forces defeat the Russians in the Battle of Smolensk.
• Lord Baltimore's settlement in Maryland was established.
• English pamphleteer William Prynne was tried and imprisoned.

> *"If my people, who are called by my name, will humble*
> *themselves and pray and seek my face and turn from*
> *their wicked ways, then I will hear from heaven,*
> *and I will forgive their sin and will heal their land."*
> 2 CHRONICLES 7:14

THE JESUS MOVEMENT

Counterculture Movement

As nose rings and tattoos are today, so long hair and hallu-cinogenic drugs were in the 1960s. Parents didn't even want to think about them. But kids—they gravitated right to them.

The hippie counterculture of the late sixties birthed crowds of spaced-out, street-living, guitar-strumming runaways. Among the disheveled souls, however, emerged revitalized Christians, often fresh from the local detox unit, who had found Jesus. They believed they stood at the cusp of a "Jesus revolution" and that the end-times were imminent. They preached on street corners, gathered a following, worshipped in jeans and T-shirts with swaying bodies and raised hands in coffeehouses, and grouped together in communes reminiscent, they imagined, of how the first Christians lived in the earliest years of the church. The Jesus Movement promised the best of both worlds: an antiestablishment statement today and eternal salvation tomorrow.

Fact: The Jesus Movement consisted largely of baby boomers, kids born after World War II. But the threat of nuclear war and the perceived hypocrisy of the middle class drove many to hippiedom.

The newly evangelized hippies' brand of religion was as far from the mainstream Protestant church of their upbringing as their lifestyle from their parents' middle-class values. Having personally "found Jesus," worshippers shunned organized religion for meetings marked by extemporaneous outpourings of praise and prayer, speaking in tongues, emotional "second blessing" baptisms, and personal spiritual experience.

Mainline ministers noticed the difference in worship styles and many added young ministers to their staff as "hippie liaisons" and incorporated more freedom of expression in their services. Members of the Jesus Movement who later cut their hair, married, and moved to the suburbs down the street from Mom and Dad tended to find their spiritual home in Pentecostal, charismatic, and evangelical congregations.

In the 1960s. . .
- Che Guevara became a symbol for revolution following his arrest and execution.
- The Algerian War ended.
- The "British Invasion" began when the Beatles arrived in America.

All the believers were together
and had everything in common.
ACTS 2:44

THE LEFT BEHIND SERIES

By Jerry B. Jenkins and Tim LaHaye (1995)

Using a specific interpretation of certain passages in 1 Corinthians, 1 Thessalonians, and the book of Revelation, authors Jerry Jenkins and Tim LaHaye created a story about the disappearance of millions of people from the earth. Frantic survivors, including airline pilot Rayford Steele, his daughter Chloe, pastor Bruce Barnes, and young journalist Cameron "Buck" Williams, search for their friends and family members only to conclude that they had been taken in the Rapture—the event marked by the coming of Jesus to snatch up His own, quietly and dramatically, as the scriptures say, like "a thief in the night."

Fact: Author Tim LaHaye based Rayford Steele, the Left Behind airline pilot, on an actual pilot LaHaye once noticed flirting with a flight attendant.

The success of the first book— *Left Behind: A Novel of the Earth's Last Days*—led to a dozen sequels, concluding with *Kingdom Come: the Final Victory* in 2007 and three prequels: *The Rising*, *The Regime*, and *The Rapture*. Readers have received all of the books with much enthusiasm.

Even though a great many Christians hold to the teaching of the Rapture as scriptural, there are a variety of theories concerning when the Rapture will actually take place. Some hold that it will happen before the period described in scripture as the "great tribulation" (Revelation 7:4 NIV). Others feel the Rapture will occur midway through the tribulation or after it ends.

The series has been criticized for many reasons including its pretribulation stance. The controversy seems to have done little to hurt sales, however, and could be credited for at least a portion of the phenomenal success of the books even with non-Christians.

In the year 1995. . .
• Jacques Chirac became president of France.
• Mississippi ratified the Thirteenth Amendment, officially abolishing slavery in the state.
• The World Trade Organization was created.

> *Listen, I tell you a mystery: We will not all sleep, but we will all be changed—in a flash, in the twinkling of an eye, at the last trumpet. For the trumpet will sound, the dead will be raised imperishable, and we will be changed.*
> 1 CORINTHIANS 15:51–52

"O FOR A THOUSAND TONGUES TO SING"

Words and Music by Charles Wesley (1739)

In May 1735, Charles and John Wesley went as missionaries to the new colony of Georgia. Onboard ship, they encountered twenty-six German Moravians, who impressed them with their hymn singing and preaching. Even during the fierce Atlantic storms, the men sang on, demonstrating to the Wesley brothers that hymn singing could be a spiritual experience and causing them to look beyond the legalistic and lifeless spirituality they had known before that time.

The mission was not deemed successful and the brothers returned within a year. Around that time, they encountered another Moravian, Peter Bohler, who expressed his spiritual joy and state of being concerning his faith by sharing the words: "Oh Brother Wesley, the Lord has done so much for my life. Had I a thousand tongues, I would praise Christ Jesus with every one of them!"

Fact: Consisting of nineteen original stanzas, this hymn is one of the longest on record.

These encounters convinced both John and Charles that they should seek more from the Christian life. They both felt they had spent too many years engaged in zealous, religious activity without ever knowing God personally or experiencing His joy.

When Charles did enter a time of deeply personal spiritual awakening, he remembered the words of the Moravian and included them in the hymn commemorating the celebration of his own conversion.

O for a thousand tongues to sing
My great Redeemer's praise,
The glories of my God and King,
The triumphs of His grace!

My gracious Master and my God,
Assist me to proclaim,
To spread through all the earth abroad
The honors of Thy name.

In the year 1749. . .
- Benning Wentworth began to develop land in what would become Vermont.
- The Ohio Company received land at the "forks" of the Ohio River to establish trade networks.
- German writer and painter Friedrich Müller was born.

Let everything that has breath praise the LORD.
Praise the LORD.
PSALM 150:6

72

ROADSIDE MEMORIALS

By the side of the highway, three white crosses stand as a solemn testament to the fragility of life.

The tradition of erecting roadside memorials for the dead is far from new. The Spanish brought to the New World their custom of using stones to mark the places between church and cemetery where pallbearers rested. Gradually, crosses replaced the stones. Within the last twenty years, roadside memorials have become an increasingly common sight along U.S. highways where fatal auto accidents have occurred, usually those involving the death of a young person. Crosses, often decorated with flowers, personal messages, teddy bears, and balloons, stand as a public expression of private grief—and a flash point for controversy.

Fact: In New York City, "ghost bikes"—old bicycles painted white—stand as memorials for cyclists who have died in crashes involving motor vehicles.

Though intended as a marker of mourning for family and friends, a memorial also can pose a distraction for motorists and an obstruction for highway maintenance crews. In addition, a vocal minority decries the presence of religious symbols on public land. States have taken various measures to meet the challenge of honoring citizens' grief and to ensure the safety and civil rights of all. A few states have banned roadside memorials altogether, while others encourage them or place a thirty-day limit on them. Other solutions to mark the scene of a fatal accident include state-sanctioned markers; wildflower gardens; an engraved brick added to an accessible state-maintained highway memorial; size and

153

placement regulations; or restriction to alcohol-related crashes only.

Passing a roadside memorial, not a few drivers remind themselves to get off the cell phone, pay attention to the road, and drive safely.

In the 1990s. . .
• North Yemen and South Yemen united.
• Margaret Thatcher resigned as Prime Minister of the United Kingdom.
• The first cloned mammal—a sheep named Dolly—was born.

Rejoice with those who rejoice;
mourn with those who mourn.
ROMANS 12:15

73

CHARLES SPURGEON

(1834–1892)
The "Prince of Preachers"

Though called the "Prince of Preachers," Englishman Charles Spurgeon was criticized for his crude and vulgar style. Behind the pulpit, he would pace the platform, act out Bible stories, and fill his sermons with melodrama about dying children, grieving parents, and repentant harlots. Spurgeon didn't listen to his critics. He said, "I must and will make people listen. My firm conviction is that we have had enough polite preachers."

His convictions created controversy along with his style. He was unwavering on theological matters and condemned ritualism, hypocrisy, and modernism. He particularly didn't like Darwinism and biblical criticism that "downgraded" the faith. The controversy took its toll on his delicate health—he experienced weight gain, bouts of gout, and depression.

Fact: Charles Spurgeon said, "If we cannot believe God when circumstances seem to be against us, we do not believe Him at all."

Once, while Spurgeon preached to a large crowd, an audience member shouted, "Fire!" and some spectators were trampled to death. Spurgeon was emotionally devastated by the event, and it had a sobering effect on his life. His faith and action kicked into high gear. He opened the massive Metropolitan Tabernacle, wrote several hymns, and challenged and befriended fellow pastors including Hudson Taylor and D. L. Moody. His sermons grew in popularity and were often published fully in the *London Times* and the *New York Times*.

Charles Spurgeon left such an impression on his fellow Englishmen that when he died, nearly sixty thousand people came to pay homage to "the preaching sensation of London" as his body lay in state. And some one hundred thousand people lined the streets during his funeral parade.

In the year 1834. . .
- Athens was established as the capital city of Greece.
- The British East India Company's trading monopoly came to an end.
- The Spanish Inquisition officially ended.

Jesus answered them, "This is the work of God, that you believe in him whom he has sent."
JOHN 6:29 ESV

HARRIET BEECHER STOWE

(1811–1896)
Abolitionist and Author of *Uncle Tom's Cabin*

Harriet Beecher Stowe was born in Litchfield, Connecticut, to Roxana Beecher and abolitionist Congregationalist preacher, Lyman Beecher. Unfortunately, Roxana died when Harriet was only four years old.

In 1832, Harriet moved with her father and two siblings, Isabella and Charles Beecher, to Cincinnati. While living in Cincinnati, Harriet experienced secondhand observations of slavery and became well acquainted with the Underground Railroad movement. She talked with former slaves as she began writing *Uncle Tom's Cabin*, the first American novel depicting an African American hero.

Harriet married widower and clergyman Calvin Ellis Stowe in 1836 and moved to Brunswick, Maine. Four of their seven children preceded her in death. When *Uncle Tom's Cabin*, her two-volume antislavery novel, was published in 1852, Harriet soon realized what her husband and readers of her articles and sketches had believed—her story had the power to change the mind. Her authentic writing about a mother's broken heart when her son was sold on the auction block came from remembering the heartache she felt when she lost her son Samuel.

Fact: When Abraham Lincoln met Harriet Beecher Stowe, he commented: "So you're the little woman who wrote the book that started this great war."

Her book sold ten thousand copies within the first week of

its release and more than three million in the first year. Within two years it had been translated into thirty-seven languages and inspired thousands to become abolitionists. *Uncle Tom's Cabin* was also among the most popular plays of the nineteenth century.

Following the Civil War, Harriet established homes for newly freed slaves. Her cause touched prominent government officials, nobility, and common people from all walks of life.

In the year 1811. . .
- Austria was forced to declare bankruptcy.
- British workers known as Luddites rioted in England against advances in technology.
- A series of earthquakes began, which a few months later in Missouri caused the Mississippi River to appear to flow upstream.

What does the LORD require of you? To act justly
and to love mercy and to walk humbly with your God.
MICAH 6:8

PATMOS

Aegean Sea

When the Roman Empire conquered the islands of the Aegean, the tiny isle of Patmos was designated as a place of exile for convicts. Its sparse vegetation, rugged terrain, and isolated location served as a natural prison. But those earthly boundaries couldn't keep the apostle John from journeying to heavenly realms. It was in Patmos, nicknamed "the Jerusalem of the Aegean," that John wrote the book of Revelation and, some theologians believe, the fourth Gospel.

Today, the Grotto of the Revelation can be found on the lowest level of the whitewashed Monastery of the Apocalypse. Both tradition and historical records support this spot as the location where John lived during his exile, from AD 84 to 96. Visitors making their way down to the grotto pass several chapels along the way, as well as a small church dedicated to "John the Theologian." The chapels were constructed in 1088, while the surrounding monastery wasn't built until the seventeenth century.

Fact: The Patmian School, which opened in 1713 on the grounds of the monastery, was the first school to officially teach Greek letters. It is now a theological seminary.

A monk is stationed at the opening of the grotto, guiding visitors down another thirteen feet into a rock grotto. Here visitors are shown the rock John used as a pillow and a cross carved into the wall, allegedly by the apostle himself. In the roof of the grotto a fissure is split into three parts, symbolic to many visitors of the Trinity. Tradition holds that this fissure is where the voice of an angel broke through the rock to tell John to write down his prophetic vision.

In the seventeenth century. . .
- Tokugawa Ieyasu founded the Tokugawa shogunate and ruled as its first shogun.
- The Gunpowder Plot—an attempt to blow up the English Parliament—failed.
- Galileo Galilei was called before the Inquisition.

Blessed is the one who reads aloud the words of this prophecy,
and blessed are those who hear it and take to heart
what is written in it, because the time is near.
REVELATION 1:3

76

THE KING JAMES BIBLE

King James I of England had reason to dislike the unauthorized but ever-popular Geneva Bible. Its decidedly Protestant leanings conflicted with the more moderate position of the Church of England. And certain marginal notes seemed to condone civil disobedience, a disturbing concept for any reigning monarch. For example, the account of Pharaoh's order that all newborn Hebrew males be killed and the midwives' refusal (Exodus 1:8–22) is accompanied by a note approving the midwives' stance. The king pronounced the commentaries of the Geneva Bible "partial, untrue, seditious, and savoring of dangerous and traitorous conceits."

In 1604, at the behest of Puritan scholar Dr. John Reynolds, the king happily authorized a new English-language Bible. Fifty-four top theologians, scholars, and experts in biblical languages assembled for the task. They divided into panels, each with particular books of the Bible to translate. Teams worked directly from Hebrew and Greek manuscripts. Completed translations were then presented to a committee of two (two translators from each panel) for review. Their purpose was to ensure that the translating panel had complied with strict rules of translation imposed on the project. In addition, the committee screened for any one translator's or team's prejudices or political leanings.

Fact: Though commissioned by King James, the Authorized King James Version of the Bible was never formally accepted by the king, nor was it ever decreed the only Bible to be read in church.

The completed work was published in 1611.

While accuracy ranked foremost in the translators' minds, they also put considerable emphasis on how the words sounded when read aloud. Their attention to this detail and their extraordinary language skill give the King James Version, or Authorized Version, of the Bible its distinctive cadence and rhythm, a quality that, in the opinion of many, remains unmatched to this day.

In the year 1611...
• Gustavus Adolphus became king of Sweden.
• Johannes Fabricius and his father discovered sunspots.
• William Shakespeare's *The Tempest* was performed in London.

The Lord is my shepherd; I shall not want. He maketh me to lie down in green pastures: he leadeth me beside the still waters.
PSALM 23:1–2 KJV

77

MERE CHRISTIANITY

By C. S. Lewis (1952)

Apologetics—the defense of the Christian faith against the assertions of empirical reasoning and scientific claims—offers informed, fact-based analyses of the Christian religion and the essential teachings of the faith. C. S. Lewis, a brilliant academic and one-time atheist, was particularly qualified to articulately address issues of belief and unbelief, and he did so with power and authority in his seminal book, *Mere Christianity*.

Mere Christianity tackles questions and objections, many involving complex spiritual concepts, that unbelievers pose to the Christian faith. He explores common reasons why unbelievers object to Christian doctrine, controversies that divide Christians from one another, and some of the stumbling blocks to faith, such as the mysteries of Holy Communion and the triune God. Lewis presents rational arguments for the reality of the God of the Bible, and from there examines Christian beliefs in a logical, clear, and accessible way. Rather than hammering his points home with dogmatic statements, Lewis offers his reasoning in a conversational manner that invites unbelievers to simply consider the idea that the tenets of the Christian faith could be true.

Fact: *Mere Christianity* is a compilation of essays Lewis read over the radio in 1943.

As Lewis completed the essays that eventually were collected in *Mere Christianity*, he sent them for review and comments to Roman Catholic, Presbyterian, Methodist, and Church of England theologians. The scholars agreed on Lewis's chief points and propositions about the Christian faith. *Mere Christianity* was enthusiastically received at its debut in 1952, and continues to this day to engage and influence Christians and non-Christians alike.

In the year 1952. . .
• Anne Frank's diary was first published in America.
• The Treaty of San Francisco between Allied and Japanese forces took effect (signed 1951).
• The term "smog" was used to describe a deadly mix of smoke and fog in London.

Always be prepared to give an answer to everyone who asks you to give the reason for the hope that you have. But do this with gentleness and respect.
1 PETER 3:15

78

"ONWARD, CHRISTIAN SOLDIERS"

Words by Sabine Baring-Gould (1865) /
Music by Arthur S. Sullivan (1871)

Sabine Baring-Gould says it took him only fifteen minutes to write the time-tested lyrics to "Onward, Christian Soldiers." Baring-Gould, squire and parson of the parish of Lewtrenchard in West Devon, England, remembers searching for music to meet a specific need.

It was the night before Whit Monday (the holiday celebrated the day after Pentecost), and Reverend Baring-Gould was planning a school festival. Children from a neighboring village had been invited, and the parson wanted the children to sing as they marched from one village to the other. Unfortunately, he could find no marching music appropriate for the occasion. Finally, he decided to write something himself. The result was this great hymn.

Originally, he entitled the piece "Hymn for Procession with Cross and Banners," and set it to a melody from Joseph Haydn's *Symphony in D, No.15.* The slow movement of the piece caused it to lag in popularity until composer Arthur Sullivan wrote a new tune for it. He entitled the melody "St. Gertrude," after the wife of a friend.

Fact: In 1986, an attempt was made to strip "Onward, Christian Soldiers" from the Methodist hymnal due to its militaristic theme. Outraged churchgoers forced the committee to back down.

"Onward, Christian Soldiers" has been sung in a number of films including *Mrs. Miniver, M*A*S*H, Taps, Flyboys,* and *A Canterbury Tale.* It was also played at the funeral of President Dwight Eisenhower.

Onward, Christian soldiers, marching as to war,
With the cross of Jesus going on before.
Christ, the royal Master, leads against the foe;
Forward into battle see His banners go!

Refrain:
Onward, Christian soldiers, marching as to war,
With the cross of Jesus going on before.

In the year 1864. . .
- Union forces under General Sherman reached Atlanta.
- Czar Alexander II enacted reforms in local government.
- "In God We Trust" appeared on U.S. coins following the Coinage Act of 1864.

Join with me in suffering,
like a good soldier of Christ Jesus.
2 TIMOTHY 2:3

79

THE TEMPERANCE MOVEMENT

America

How could I ever think to wed
A man who's always drunken;
Who really has so large a head,
It looks like a ripe pumpkin.

A swell-headed, bottle-toting gentleman in the illustration accompanying this poem from an 1860s woodcut looks like a poor marriage prospect, and that's the point. Choose for yourselves, men: the bottle or a bride.

The temperance movement in the United States began to take shape in the late eighteenth century after the publication of Dr. Benjamin Rush's moral thermometer. The Philadelphia physician illustrated degrees of drunkenness by beverage and its effects. According to the moral thermometer, pepper in rum, the worst beverage, led to suicide, death, and the gallows. Water, the best beverage, brought health, wealth, serenity of mind, reputation, long life, and happiness.

Fact: In the late 1800s, T. S. Arthur's temperance book, *Ten Nights in a Bar-Room,* ranked second only to *Uncle Tom's Cabin* in sales.

By the mid-nineteenth century, temperance organizations attracted men and women of all races, classes, and religious leanings with around one million members. Vocal temperance advocates lobbied for federal and state restraints on the increasingly profitable alcohol trafficking business. In 1851, Maine lawmakers declared the entire state of Maine "dry." Other states followed with laws limiting or prohibiting alcohol sale and consumption.

Women proved a formidable force within the temperance movement. In 1874, they organized the Woman's Christian Temperance Union (WCTU), advocating total abstinence from alcohol because of its destructive effects on health and family life. The WCTU and other all-female organizations became the political "training grounds" of several later prominent suffragists.

The movement lost popular attention during the years of the Civil War, though its influence continued through the Prohibition Party in the early twentieth century.

In the eighteenth century. . .
- Napoleon Bonaparte became first consul following a coup d'état in Paris.
- The Dutch East India Company dissolved.
- The first smallpox vaccination was administered by Edward Jenner.

Let us behave decently, as in the daytime, not in carousing and drunkenness, not in sexual immorality and debauchery, not in dissension and jealousy.
ROMANS 13:13

80

BILLY SUNDAY

(1862–1935)
Baseball Player and Evangelist

During his first professional baseball at-bat, Billy Sunday struck out! In that very same game, he would strike out two more times. He would go on to strike out seven times and see three more games before he finally got his first hit. Undeterred, Sunday became one of the most popular players in the game in the late 1800s. He played for the Chicago White Sox, the Pittsburgh Pirates, and the Philadelphia Athletics.

Fact: Throughout his preaching career, Sunday remained prominent in baseball, umpiring minor league games and even attending the 1935 World Series two months before he died.

Sunday's start in life didn't predict success in anything. Five weeks after he was born, his Civil War veteran father died. When Billy was ten, his mother was forced to send him and his siblings to a soldier's orphanage because she couldn't afford to take care of them. Nevertheless, Billy gained a high school education and discovered great athletic skill.

While playing major league baseball, in 1886, Billy stopped by the Pacific Garden Mission in Chicago and there was converted to Christianity. He immediately began preaching in churches and at YMCAs. In fact, Billy would turn down a lucrative baseball contract to accept a position with the Chicago YMCA for two-thirds the pay—just to preach!

After conducting a revival in Iowa, Sunday held campaigns throughout the Midwest. After World War I, he preached in

Boston, New York, and other major cities. Unorthodox in his style, he would often cuss, use colorful language, and prance around the stage—sometimes even throwing chairs. He firmly stood against card-playing, movie-going, and especially drinking alcohol. He remains one of the most colorful and successful evangelists in American history.

In the year 1862. . .
• The USS *Monitor* became the first ironclad ship in the American Civil War.
• Otto von Bismarck became Prime Minister of Prussia.
• The Battle of Antietam was fought near Sharpsburg, Maryland.

I have strength for all things in Christ Who empowers me [I am ready for anything and equal to anything through Him Who infuses inner strength into me; I am self-sufficient in Christ's sufficiency.]
PHILIPPIANS 4:13 AMP

81

CORRIE TEN BOOM

(1892–1983)
Missionary and Evangelist

At age fifty, Cornelia ten Boom found herself in the middle of a national crisis that changed her life forever. As war ravaged Germany she prayed, "Lord Jesus, I offer myself for Your people. In any way. Any place. Any time."

Within days of Cornelia's prayer, she and her family, living in the Netherlands, became an integral part of an underground rescue mission. Offering refuge from racial persecution to all who knocked on their door, her family's home soon became a safe hiding place.

In February of 1944, a trusted friend told the Gestapo that the ten Booms were harboring fugitive Jews. The entire family was arrested and imprisoned in the Ravensbrück concentration camp, where Corrie lost her father, a nephew, and eventually her beloved sister, Betsy. Before Betsy's death, the sisters spent much of their time ministering God's love through His Word to the other inmates. At great risk, they smuggled in Bibles and translated the Dutch Bible into German.

Fact: Corrie ten Boom traveled to more than sixty countries, sharing her story of love, forgiveness, and restoration, and published eighteen books. *The Hiding Place* sold in excess of a million copies.

Due to a clerical error in 1945, Corrie ten Boom was released. She later learned that one week after her release, all other women her age had been executed in the gas chambers. "I knew my life had been given back for a purpose.... I was no longer my own," Corrie stated.

In 1945, Corrie set up a ministry for the war-damaged people of Holland in Bloemendaal—a donated mansion. She later renovated a German concentration camp and opened her own father's house for refugees.

In the year 1892. . .
- The first immigrants entered Ellis Island.
- Sir Arthur Conan Doyle published his collection of Sherlock Holmes stories.
- Work began on the Trans-Siberian Railroad.

Yet he did not waver through unbelief regarding the promise of God, but was strengthened in his faith and gave glory to God.
ROMANS 4:20

82

PLYMOUTH ROCK

Plymouth, Massachusetts

It's hard to believe a rock could be so revered—especially one in such bad shape. But Plymouth Rock, traditionally believed to be the site where the Pilgrims disembarked from the Mayflower after their sixty-five-day sea voyage from Plymouth, England, is venerated as a memorial to those who were courageous in the face of religious persecution.

The people we traditionally call "pilgrims" referred to themselves as Puritan Separatists. They "separated" from the Church of England because they believed the church was not fulfilling the work of the Reformation Martin Luther had set in motion. Facing ongoing persecution, 102 Puritans chose to sail to the New World to start a British colony—all this in the hope that they would be able to freely live out their faith.

Fact: Plymouth Rock has been moved several times, cracking and breaking apart in the process. And throughout the years, people have also chipped off pieces to take as souvenirs.

Their dream came at a high price. The Mayflower was overcrowded and the seas were rough. On the crossing, two people died and two babies were born. But many of the Pilgrims were sick when they arrived at the end of December 1620. By spring, more than forty of their small group had perished. But working together with the Wampanoag Indians, the Puritans carved out a home where their faith could thrive. Years later, their leader, William Bradford, wrote, "Thus, out of small beginnings. . . as one small candle may light a thousand, so the light here kindled hath shone unto many, yea in some sort to our whole nation, let the glorious name of Jehovah have all the praise."

In the year 1620. . .
- Germany declared neutrality in the Treaty of Ulm (Thirty Years' War).
- Francis Bacon published his work on logical thinking, *Novum Organum*.
- Inventor Cornelius Drebbel experimented with an underwater boat in the Thames.

Who shall separate us from the love of Christ? Shall trouble or hardship or persecution or famine or nakedness or danger or sword?
ROMANS 8:35

83

MICHELANGELO PAINTS THE SISTINE CHAPEL

Vatican City

An accomplished sculptor, Michelangelo had not lifted a paintbrush beyond his student days. That is, until Pope Julius II requested his services to paint the vaulted ceiling of the restored Sistine Chapel. A pope's personal invitation is not something lightly dismissed.

The work took more than four years to complete. The ceiling, about 131 feet long by 43 feet wide, required more than 4,000 square feet of frescoes (paint applied to damp plaster). Nine scenes from the book of Genesis, from the Creation of the world to the Flood, form a center column that runs the length of the ceiling. On the sides are portraits of the Old Testament prophets who foretold the coming of the Christ. Portraits and scenes along the upper part of the walls depict the history of ancient Israel. Decorative cherubs and Sibyls float throughout. Overall, more than three hundred painted figures grace the ceiling.

Fact: Despite scenes from the movies and popular perception, Michelangelo probably didn't paint the ceiling while lying on his back.

Although Michelangelo designed and sketched the cartoons and painted almost every inch of the frescoes, numerous assistants took part in the project. They prepared the plaster, mixed paints, and delivered tools and material to the artist perched atop the scaffolding. Occasionally, a senior assistant painted an inconsequential figure or minute patch of scenery. Michelangelo is known to have fired assistants at a moment's notice, however, not allowing any one painter cause to credit himself with even a small part of the magnificent work.

Michelangelo completed his masterpiece in October of 1512, and Pope Julius marked the occasion with a solemn mass on November 1, the Feast of All Saints.

In the year 1512...
- The Medici family regained power in Florence.
- Martin Luther attended the University of Wittenberg.
- Copernicus wrote his theories on a sun-centered solar system in *Commentariolus.*

> LORD, *I love the house where you live,*
> *the place where your glory dwells.*
> PSALM 26:8

THE PRACTICE OF THE PRESENCE OF GOD

By Brother Lawrence (c. 1691)

Brother Lawrence, a seventeenth-century Carmelite monk, yearned to live every moment of his day in the presence of God. He aspired to a habitual state of holy communion that would draw no distinction between times of work and times of prayer, times for chores and times for worship. During his lifetime, his reputation as a gifted mystic and spiritual counselor drew devoted students and followers. After the monk's death in 1691, one of his disciples collected his letters and transcriptions of conversations into the spiritual classic *The Practice of the Presence of God*.

The key to communion with God, Brother Lawrence proposed, rests in the faithful practice of spiritual discipline. In *The Practice of the Presence of God*, he describes three degrees of union of the soul with God (general, virtual, and actual) and outlines techniques to reach each level, including unceasing worship, setting one's mind on God at all times, and acceptance of whatever conditions and circumstances life brings.

Fact: In his role as cook for his monastery, Brother Lawrence referred to himself as "the lord of pots and pans."

He spent his lifetime in a continual effort to get closer to God by attaining ever higher levels of perfection in thought and action. His stellar conduct, focused mind, and deepening knowledge of the divine, he believed, would assure him the communion he sought so earnestly. Despite the human effort required, Brother Lawrence humbly attributed to God any degree of progress he achieved.

Today, committed Christians recognize, as Brother Lawrence did, the link between religion of the heart and religion as it is lived out in the mundane activities of daily life. Christianity not practiced in the real world is, in essence, Christianity not practiced at all.

In the year 1691. . .
- The Treaty of Limerick secured some civil rights for Irish Catholics.
- Leisler's Rebellion ended with the arrest of Jacob Leisler.
- Michel Rolle developed his mathematical theory called Rolle's Theorem.

So whether you eat or drink or whatever you do,
do it all for the glory of God.
1 CORINTHIANS 10:31

"SILENT NIGHT"

Words by Joseph Mohr (c. 1816–1818)
English Translation: John F. Young (1863)
Music by Franz Grüber (1820)

The beautiful carol "Silent Night" was much more than a casual inspiration; it was the miraculous answer to prayer.

A young priest named Joseph Mohr was preparing a special Christmas Eve service one unusually cold night when he noticed that the church organ was not working. He did his best to get the old instrument operating again, but to no avail. Uncertain what to do, he paused to pray. It was then that he remembered a Christmas poem he had written several years earlier. He had played with a few melodies, shared it with a few friends, but never sought to have it published.

Fact: A manuscript has been found that seems to indicate that the music for "Silent Night" was written by Grüber, but two to four years later. This much-told story could be simply folklore.

Mohr pulled the poem from a desk drawer, bundled up, and hurried out into the cold. Just a few hours before the service was to begin, he sought help from his friend, schoolteacher and composer Franz Grüber. Mohr asked the surprised man if he could write music for his poem in the hours left before the Christmas Eve service. Not only did Grüber accomplish the task, but with time to teach it to the choir. Accompanied by Mohr on the guitar, the simple melody filled the church.

The story of how the song was written traveled quickly, and its popularity skyrocketed. An Austrian singing group carried the melody to New York, where it was well received. "Silent Night" has now been recorded more than any other song in history.

> *Silent night, holy night,*
> *All is calm, all is bright.*
> *Round yon virgin mother and child.*
> *Holy infant, so tender and mild,*
> *Sleep in heavenly peace,*
> *Sleep in heavenly peace.*

In the year 1818. . .
- Mary Shelley's novel *Frankenstein* was published.
- Paul Revere died.
- The U.S. Congress adopted the practice of adding one star to the flag for each new state.

> *[The angel said,] "This will be the sign to you: You will*
> *find a Babe wrapped in swaddling cloths, lying in a manger."*
> LUKE 2:12 NKJV

A THIEF IN THE NIGHT

The Movie

What would it be like to wake up one morning and find that millions of people—every single one of them Christian—have suddenly disappeared? Such is the setting for the first Rapture movie, *A Thief in the Night*. Issued in 1972, the widely acclaimed suspense saga and its three sequels (*A Distant Thunder*, *Image of the Beast*, and *Prodigal Planet*) depict events as they unfold in the years prior to Christ's Second Coming. They draw on the language and symbols of biblical prophecies, especially those found in the book of Revelation.

For two millennia, mysterious passages of perhaps the Bible's most mysterious book have set imaginations working overtime to construct an end-times scenario. Speculations include a one-thousand-year earthly reign of Jesus Christ, marked by perfect peace and prosperity on earth. Another theory depicts a "rapture"—the taking up of Christians into heaven—followed by great suffering on earth initiated by a malevolent figure, the antichrist. Then Christ's one-thousand-year reign begins, after which the devil roams once more until the Battle of Armageddon and final judgment. Some—or a combination—of these events embraced by many conservative Christians served as the starting point for *A Thief in the Night* and subsequent end-times movies and books.

Fact: During filming, actress Patty Dunning slipped on a railroad trestle and almost fell through the cracks. Her experience as a professional gymnast may have helped her avoid a sixty-foot fall.

Apocalyptic speculation reached its peak in the years leading up to the dawn of the third millennium. "Prophets" predicted everything from the release of virulent computer worms to the coming of Jesus Christ at one minute past midnight on December 31, 1999. The moment passed without incident. There are some things that must remain a mystery until—the end-times.

In the year 1972. . .
• India and Bangladesh sign a treaty of friendship.
• Japan regained control of Okinawa after decades of military occupation.
• The last trolleybus system closed in the United Kingdom.

"If the owner of the house had known at what time of night the thief was coming, he would have kept watch and would not have let his house be broken into. So you also must be ready, because the Son of Man will come at an hour when you do not expect him."
MATTHEW 24:43–44

HUDSON TAYLOR

(1832–1905)
Founder of China Inland Mission (CIM)

From a very early age, Hudson Taylor seemed destined to be a missionary in China. His Methodist parents were fascinated by the Far East and they prayed over him as a newborn, "God, grant that he might work for You in China." During his teen years, Taylor studied medicine, the Bible, and the Mandarin language. At age twenty-one, Taylor was bound on a clipper ship for Shanghai.

Immediately, Taylor decided to make himself distinct from the Western missionaries he saw there. He decided to dress in Chinese clothes and grow the braid typical Chinese men wore. He also decided to venture into the Chinese interior, sailing down the Huangpu River, distributing Chinese Bibles and tracts.

After the Chinese Evangelization Society said it couldn't pay him as a missionary, he decided to become an independent missionary, trusting God to provide his every need.

Fact: Hudson Taylor wrote, "You must first go forward on your knees."

After an illness and a return to England, Taylor established an ambitious plan to bring missionaries to China. His own vision left him racked with doubt, but he was convinced of God's love for the Chinese. He formed a group called the China Inland Mission (CIM) and returned to China with even a greater fervor than he had on his initial trip.

For all his lifelong effort in China (fifty-one years), Taylor brought more than eight hundred missionaries to the country, who began 125 schools, which directly resulted in eighteen

183

thousand Christian conversions. His work also established more than three bases and five local helpers in all eighteen provinces. All this occurred before his death in China at age seventy-three.

In the year 1832...
• The Black Hawk War began across Illinois and Michigan Territory.
• The New England Anti-Slavery Society was organized.
• Durham University was founded.

To those who are weak, I became weak so I could win the weak. I have become all things to all people so I could save some of them in any way possible.
1 CORINTHIANS 9:22 NCV

88

SOJOURNER TRUTH

(1797–1883)
Abolitionist and Feminist

That man over there says that women need to be helped into carriages, and lifted over ditches, and to have the best place everywhere. Nobody ever helps me into carriages, or over mud puddles, or gives me any best place, and ain't I a woman?" In 1854, those words rang out from a remarkable woman.

Born a slave in upstate New York, Isabella Baumfree endured a succession of heartless owners in her early years. As a teenager, she bore a daughter by a fellow slave but was forced to marry one her master chose. Promised her freedom in 1826, a year before state emancipation was to take effect, Isabella left the house when her master reneged on his promise.

Fact: A twelve-foot statue of Sojourner Truth will grace Monument Park in Battle Creek, Michigan, where she lived for more than twenty years.

Isabella arrived at the home of a couple who bought her services from her master. During this time, she experienced "the greatness of the Divine presence." She began attending the Methodist church, eventually traveling as an itinerant preacher and at times joining groups of like-minded believers. On June 1, 1843, Isabella changed her name to Sojourner Truth and resolved to continue traveling, preaching, and depending on the hospitality of strangers for her food and shelter.

Later, the publication of her memoirs provided an income and opened speaking opportunities. A charismatic woman, Sojourner spoke eloquently on women's rights, pacifism, and the abolition of slavery. During the Civil War, she worked among freed slaves at a government refugee camp.

The Mars Pathfinder Sojourner Rover is named after a woman who spoke the earthly (and celestial) truth.

In the year 1797...
- The British were victorious against the Spanish in the Battle of Cape St. Vincent.
- The XYZ Affair developed between France and the United States.
- Napoleon Bonaparte conquered Rivoli.

For the one who was a slave when called to faith
in the Lord is the Lord's freed person; similarly,
the one who was free when called is Christ's slave.
1 CORINTHIANS 7:22

89

QUMRAN CAVES

Israel

One of the greatest manuscript discoveries of modern times might never have happened if it weren't for a stray goat. In 1947, two Bedouin cousins were throwing rocks onto the cave-riddled hillsides of Israel's Judean wilderness, trying to startle a wayward goat out of hiding. But instead of hearing a goat's bleat, the boys heard pottery shatter. Muhammed ehd-Dhib, nicknamed "the Wolf," climbed up into a small cave to investigate. There he found lidded jars containing ancient scrolls.

After Wolf's discovery, both archaeologists and thieves began scouring the surrounding hills. By 1956, eleven caves had been found, containing about 850 scrolls. From tens of thousands of fragments, two hundred separate books written in Hebrew, Aramaic, and Greek as early as 250 BC were recovered from the Qumran Caves. The manuscripts include hymnals, sermons, rules of warfare, and commentaries on Hebrew scripture. But the most significant find is 122 handwritten copies of books of the Old Testament. Every book is represented except Esther. Aside from a few spelling and verb tense errors, the scripture written on the scrolls is in substantial agreement with modern-day translations of the Bible.

Fact: All of the Dead Sea Scrolls are written on animal skins or papyrus, except for one. It's incised on a thin sheet of copper.

The Isaiah Scroll (one of twenty-four copies of Isaiah found in the Qumran Caves) is considered one of the most important manuscript finds in history. Found virtually intact, this manuscript is more than a thousand years older than any previously known copy of Isaiah. The manuscript is currently housed in the Shrine of the Book Museum in Jerusalem.

In the year 1947. . .
- Britain and France signed the Treaty of Dunkirk, pledging mutual aid should Germany rearm.
- Jackie Robinson became the first African American major league baseball player since 1889.
- A UFO was sighted at Roswell, New Mexico.

He will be the sure foundation for your times,
a rich store of salvation and wisdom and knowledge;
the fear of the LORD is the key to this treasure.
ISAIAH 33:6

MISSIONARIES MASSACRED

Ecuador (1956)

Jim Elliot was a gifted writer, speaker, and teacher. In fact, he excelled in most everything, including sports. Those who knew him, however, pointed to extraordinary spiritual depth as his defining characteristic. Everyone expected him to one day contribute to the advancement of the American church. But Elliot had something different in mind.

After much prayer, Elliot felt called to the mission field, specifically South America. Through a friend, formerly a missionary to Ecuador, he learned of the fierce Auca tribe deep in the jungle and unreached by the gospel. The Aucas had a murderous history—two Shell Oil employees had fallen into their hands and were killed.

Fact: In 2006, the movie *End of the Spear* told the story of pilot Nate Saint and followed his son's journey back to Ecuador and a reunion with the Aucas he had known as a child.

In 1955, while ministering to the Quichua Indians, Elliot saw a chance to reach the Aucas when Nate Saint, a missionary pilot, spotted an Auca village from the air. For several months, the men dropped gifts from the plane in an attempt to befriend the villagers. In January of 1956, Elliot, Saint, and three others landed on the beach near the village. Two days later, all five of the brave, young missionaries were attacked with spears and killed.

In the years that followed, other missionaries, including Jim Elliot's wife, Elisabeth, and Nate Saint's sister, Rachel, reached out to the Aucas, and many came to Christ. *Life* magazine featured a ten-page article on the incident, and Elisabeth Elliot's books

Shadow of the Almighty and *Through Gates of Splendor* chronicled her husband's life and ministry. The story of the five missionaries to the Aucas stirred the hearts of many and created a boon for Christian missions around the world.

In the year 1956. . .
• Morocco became independent.
• Nasser nationalized the Suez Canal, prompting the Suez Crisis between Egypt and Britain.
• Japan joined the United Nations.

Because of the service by which you have proved yourselves, others will praise God for the obedience that accompanies your confession of the gospel of Christ.
2 CORINTHIANS 9:13

THE PURPOSE DRIVEN LIFE

By Rick Warren (2002)

"Why on earth am I here?" That's the question megachurch pastor Rick Warren sets out to answer in his megaselling book, *The Purpose Driven Life*. With more than eighteen million copies sold since its publication in 2002, the book has become an influential force in contemporary-Christian thinking worldwide.

In forty chapters, intended to be read on forty consecutive days, Warren challenges readers to take each inspirational thought he offers and make it their own. He leads readers to conform their lives around God's plan for them as individuals, as opposed to trying to manipulate God into granting personal favors. The book's program of discovery and discernment is founded on Warren's discovery of five God-given purposes for each person's life. He cites these purposes as to: love God with all your heart; love your neighbor as yourself; make disciples (evangelism); join and participate in a church; and teach others.

Fact: A spate of associated journals, study guides, meditations, and calendars followed the success of *The Purpose Driven Life*, in addition to sequels targeting specific groups of readers.

In each concise chapter, Warren expounds on a single aspect of Christian living in positive, upbeat language. With references to contemporary culture, the Southern Baptist pastor reaches out to Christians who may not be versed in biblical imagery and doctrinal arguments. Critics complain that Warren avoids some of the more difficult truths of Christianity, such as sin, hell, and judgment. While certainly not a complete course on Christianity,

The Purpose Driven Life achieves its purpose of getting the general reader and ordinary Christian to interact with his or her faith in a personal, observable, and meaningful way.

In the year 2002. . .
• Civil war began in Côte d'Ivoire.
• The United States invaded Afghanistan in Operation Anaconda.
• NASA's Mars Odyssey prepared to map the surface of Mars.

> *They asked him, "What must we do to do the works*
> *God requires?" Jesus answered, "The work of God is this:*
> *to believe in the one he has sent."*
> JOHN 6:28–29

"TRUST AND OBEY"

Words by John H. Sammis (1887)
Music by Daniel B. Towner (1887)

John H. Sammis became a young, successful New York businessman at age twenty-three. When he moved to Logansport, Indiana, to pursue his career, he also became active as a Christian layman. Some time later, he gave up his business career, became the YMCA secretary, and answered a call to full-time ministry. He attended McCormick and Lane Theological seminaries, graduated from Lane in 1881, and was ordained as a Presbyterian minister. In the following years he served as pastor in churches in Iowa, Indiana, Michigan, and Minnesota.

Fact: D. L. Moody said, "The blood alone makes us safe, the Word alone makes us sure, but obedience alone makes us happy."

In 1886, during a service in Brockton, Massachusetts, where he was leading music for D. L. Moody, Daniel B. Towner heard a young man's testimony and jotted down his words: "I am not quite sure—but I am going to trust, and I am going to obey." Mr. Towner sent the words he'd written down to Reverend Sammis, and the great hymn "Trust and Obey" was born. It first appeared in *Hymns Old and New*, published in 1887.

This favorite gospel hymn ranks as an excellent example of balance in the life of a believer between faith in Christ and good works that should naturally occur if one takes to heart the words of trusting and obeying Christ in daily living.

When we walk with the Lord in the light of His Word,
What a glory He sheds on our way!
While we do His good will, He abides with us still,
And with all who will trust and obey.

Refrain:
Trust and obey, for there's no other way
To be happy in Jesus, but to trust and obey.

In the year 1887. . .
- Massive flooding occurred around the Yellow River in China.
- The Dawes Act allowed the U.S. government to divide Indian reservation land.
- Work began in Paris on the Eiffel Tower (completed in 1889).

Samuel replied: "Does the LORD delight in burnt offerings and sacrifices as much as in obeying the LORD? To obey is better than sacrifice, and to heed is better than the fat of rams."
1 SAMUEL 15:22

VeggieTales

Verbal Vegetables

What's the big idea? The gospel as told by a tomato, Bob, and a cucumber, Larry, that's what. Computer animator Phil Vischer's first half-hour episode, *Where's God When I'm S–S–Scared?* debuted in late 1993 as the nation's first completely computer-animated video. The kids—and parents—loved it.

Vischer founded his media company, Big Idea, with the goal of creating family-friendly films with Christian themes. He and his cocreator, Mike Nawrocki, produced a series of half-hour videos based on biblical themes, many of them suggested by letters from fans. Episodes begin as Bob and Larry ponder a moral dilemma and talk it over with other vegetables. When no one can come up with a firm answer, everyone agrees to discover what the Bible says about the issue and they "roll the video." Bob and Larry close the show with a moral and an applicable Bible verse.

Fact: Before airing VeggieTales, NBC edited out all mention of God and other specifically religious words. After strong criticism from Vischer and fans, the network stopped.

In 2002, Big Idea came to the big screen with *Jonah—A VeggieTales Movie,* one of the most successful general audience films of the year. Lively animation and deft screenwriting supported goofy humor and catchy songs kids and adults could enjoy. The creators, through their choice of voices and vegetables, brought in a broad diversity of races, ethnic origins, accents, and body shapes.

Despite the remarkable growth and sunny sales of Big Idea productions, the company died on the vine in 2003. It has since been purchased by other media companies. In the fall of 2006, *Veggie Tales* episodes were released on national television.

In the year 1993. . .
• Czechoslovakia became Slovakia and the Czech Republic.
• The first direct presidential elections were held in Mongolia.
• Public visitors were allowed to tour Buckingham Palace for the first time.

> *As the soil makes the sprout come up and a garden causes seeds to grow, so the Sovereign LORD will make righteousness and praise spring up before all nations.*
> ISAIAH 61:11

JOHN WESLEY

(1703–1791)
Early Methodist Leader

In late 1735, on board a ship bound for America, the young Anglican minister John Wesley and his fellow passengers encountered a fierce storm. Though he was chaplain of the vessel, Wesley feared for the lives of the passengers. As the ship tossed about on the ferocious waves, he noticed a group of German Moravians quietly singing hymns below deck. Impressed, Wesley asked the leader of the group about the nature of his calm serenity. The German replied, "Do you have faith in Christ?" Though Wesley replied that he did, he wondered if his words were spoken in vain.

This event served to strengthen Wesley as he believed the grace of Christ was issued on the practices (or disciplines) of prayer, scripture reading, meditation, Holy Communion, and charitable acts such as prison visitation, etc. These methods of "Christian Perfection" became known as Methodism and were the means by which the Christian believer became transformed.

Fact: John Wesley wrote, "The world is my parish."

As Methodism continued to organize, Wesley remained in the Anglican Church and rallied his followers with these words: "Do all the good you can, by all the means you can, in all the ways you can, in all the places you can, at all the times you can, to all the people you can, as long as ever you can." Wesley joined George Whitefield, and together the two took Methodism to greater organization and prominence.

John Wesley's teachings also influenced the holiness movement, from which came Pentecostalism and the Charismatic movement.

In the year 1703...
• Peter the Great founded St. Petersburg in Russia.
• Despite intending to remain neutral in Spanish Succession, Portugal joined the Grand Alliance.
• Daniel Defoe was imprisoned for his satirical pamphlets.

Trust in the LORD, and do good; so shalt thou
dwell in the land, and verily thou shalt be fed.
PSALM 37:3 KJV

95

JULIAN OF NORWICH

(1342–1416)
Writer and Christian Mystic

Poor harvests. Widespread hunger. A disintegrating social order. The Black Plague hanging in the air. The church embroiled in internal strife. In an age of conflict, fear, and unrest, Julian of Norwich was celebrated for her message of God's love and eternal hope.

Little is known about the English mystic's life except that she took the vows of a Benedictine nun in Norwich's St. Julian Church, from which she took her name. For the rest of her years, she lived as an *anchorite*—one who lives in a fixed place and in solitude for the purpose of attaining religious perfection. Julian resided in a small room attached to the church, where she devoted herself to prayer, meditation, and intellectual development. Though a recluse, she provided spiritual counsel to those who sought her out and became known for her gentle wisdom and spiritual insights. Julian's keen religious perception led her to express genuine joy despite the hardships and uncertainties of her time. Her expressions of God's enduring love and friendship gave hope and encouragement to her followers, who heard nothing but God's condemnation and wrath from the pulpit.

Fact: Julian of Norwich wrote, "Just as our flesh is covered by clothing, and our blood is covered by our flesh, so are we, soul and body, covered and enclosed by the goodness of God."

The first known female writer in English, Julian penned *Revelations of Divine Love*. Written after her recovery from a life-threatening illness, *Revelations of Divine Love* is based on sixteen "showings," or visions, of Christ she received while ill. In lively and descriptive prose, she reveals a sound knowledge of church doctrine along with profound spiritual perception. *Revelations of Divine Love* is considered a masterpiece of English literature.

In the year 1343. . .
- Pope Clement VI issued a papal bull *Unigenitus* concerning indulgences.
- Estonians rebelled against foreign landlords in the St. George's Uprising.
- Geoffrey Chaucer was born.

> *Give thanks to the LORD, for he is good.*
> *His love endures forever.*
> PSALM 136:1

96

WAILING WALL

Jerusalem

King Solomon built Israel's first permanent temple around 960 BC. The Babylonians razed the temple in 586 BC, but a second temple was built around 515 when Persia, which had conquered Babylon, allowed Jews to return to Jerusalem.

Fact: The largest stone built into the Western Wall weighs approximately 570 tons. In contrast, the largest stone in the Great Pyramid of Egypt weighs only 11 tons.

Centuries later, Herod the Great built a third temple on the same site as the earlier two. But in AD 70, the Roman Empire destroyed the temple once more, leaving just the western wall standing. The Romans wanted the wall to be a bittersweet reminder to the Jews, a symbol that Rome was the ultimate conqueror. However, the Jewish people did not see the wall as a monument to Rome's victory, but to God's faithfulness. His temple stood fast, just like His unbroken bond with His people.

Today, the Wailing Wall (so nicknamed because of all those who've mourned the destruction of the temple at this site) continues to be a place of both battles and prayer. The area is considered sacred to Jews, Christians, and Muslims. In 1929, the League of Nations declared that the wall and surrounding area was owned by the Muslims, but that Jews should have free access to worship there at all times.

Today, visitors of all religions are invited to approach the wall in silent prayer. In keeping with Jewish tradition, there is a divider separating men and women while they pray. Many visitors write their prayers on pieces of paper, which they then place in crevices on the wall. This practice has been around for hundreds of years, since Jewish tradition says the gate of heaven itself lies directly above the Western Wall.

In the year 1929. . .
• Vatican City became a sovereign state.
• The Treaty of Lima settled border disputes between Peru and Chile.
• Herbert Hoover became the thirty-first president of the United States.

We are the temple of the living God.
2 CORINTHIANS 6:16

THE SCOPES TRIAL

Street banners, lemonade stands, and performing chimpanzees. Over a thousand onlookers, in addition to reporters and journalists from far and wide, swarmed the streets of Dayton, Tennessee, in July of 1925, to witness a trial billed as a showdown between good and evil, truth and ignorance.

High school biology teacher John T. Scopes was accused of presenting Darwin's theory of evolution in a public school classroom in violation of the Butler Act, an antievolution state law. The "Monkey Trial," catering to the popular understanding of evolution as meaning human beings descended directly from apes, was in full swing. Criminal lawyer Clarence Darrow represented Scopes, and former U.S. Secretary of State William Jennings Bryan appeared for the prosecution. Darrow argued for the validity of evolution and the unconstitutionality of the Butler Act. Bryan spoke passionately in defense of the biblical account of creation.

Fact: The 1920s were a time of social upheaval, pitting young, "progressive" thinkers against fundamentalists and social conservatives, especially in the South.

The trial was far from an intellectual, or even religious, debate. Darrow, Bryan, and Judge John T. Raulston, each for his own reasons, craved publicity and encouraged monkeyshines. Through day-by-day radio broadcasts, the Monkey Trial and its colorful courtroom antics sparked debate in cafés, beauty salons, and barbershops from coast to coast. The trial ended when the jury found Scopes guilty and the court fined him one hundred dollars.

The state supreme court reversed the verdict on technical

grounds, though the Butler Act remained on the books until 1967. Debate on the teaching of evolution in public school classrooms versus the Creation account in the book of Genesis continues in state legislatures and courtrooms to this day.

In the year 1925. . .
• F. Scott Fitzgerald published his novel *The Great Gatsby*.
• Excavation was completed on the Great Sphinx at Giza.
• The first radio broadcasts began of what would evolve into the Grand Ole Opry.

> *God created mankind in his own image, in the image of God he created them; male and female he created them.*
> GENESIS 1:27

THIS PRESENT DARKNESS

By Frank E. Peretti (1986)

Do we live our lives unaware of a second, invisible reality always moving around us, influencing us for evil or for good? That's the platform for Frank Peretti's groundbreaking novel, *This Present Darkness*.

The novel's chief protagonist is a godly pastor by the name of Hank Busche, who discovers a sinister plot to turn Ashton's college into a bulwark of New Age philosophy. Falsely discredited and facing death threats, Hank and his wife, Mary, go to prayer and cause heavenly forces to be deployed on their behalf. As the plot flips back and forth from earthly realm to heavenly realm, Peretti gives the reader a bird's-eye view of the action.

Fact: The sequel to *This Present Darkness*, entitled *Piercing the Darkness*, was published in 1988.

For a great many Christians, *This Present Darkness* brought to life a concept that had heretofore been vague and undefined. Creatures from the spiritual world now had both face and persona. They could be acknowledged and addressed.

Of course, the novel was not without its detractors. Some literary critics argued that the characters were simplistically typecast in roles of good and evil. Some theological critics argued that the biblical metaphor of spiritual warfare has everything to do with the struggle of the soul against sin and nothing to do with combat between angels and demons. Others simply remind readers that the book is fantasy rather than biblical scholarship; this is based on, among other things, the inclusion of female angels, baby angels, and pip-squeak demons, which have no basis in scripture.

Regardless of how some authorities view the book, there is no denying its success with readers. The book has sold more than 2.5 million copies worldwide.

In the year 1986. . .
- The crew of *Challenger* died when the space shuttle broke apart during its flight.
- The Statue of Liberty reopened to the public after restoration work was completed.
- Elie Wiesel won the Nobel Peace Prize.

Our struggle is not against flesh and blood, but against the rulers, against the authorities, against the powers of this dark world and against the spiritual forces of evil in the heavenly realms.
EPHESIANS 6:12

"WHEN THE ROLL IS CALLED UP YONDER"

Words and Music by James M. Black (1893)

James M. Black, a Methodist layman, music teacher, composer, and publisher of numerous gospel songs, found his inspiration for this hymn during a consecration meeting. He had invited a downtrodden fourteen-year-old girl to the meeting, and when members repeated scriptures as they answered roll call, he noticed she was absent—and therefore did not respond. As he thought of how sad it would be if names were called from the Lamb's Book of Life without receiving a response, the first words to the first stanza of this hymn were birthed. Within a few minutes, he composed two more verses. When he sat down at the piano to compose a tune for the hymn, the notes formed the melody still found in hymnbooks today.

Fact: "When the Roll Is Called Up Yonder" is harmonized with just four basic chords.

The girl who inspired those first words died of pneumonia shortly thereafter. Her death furnished the dramatic finale to the hymn and gives credence to the roll-call song.

Since its publication, the simple words have planted seeds of promise for a glorious future in the hearts of believers. After the hymn first appeared in Black's most popular hymnbook, *Songs of the Soul*, published in 1894—a hymnal that sold more than four hundred thousand copies in its first two years—it soon became widely used in evangelistic meetings in Great Britain and the United States.

When the trumpet of the Lord shall sound,
And time shall be no more,
And the morning breaks, eternal, bright and fair;
When the saved of earth
Shall gather over on the other shore,
And the roll is called up yonder, I'll be there.

In the year 1894. . .
- Mahatma Gandhi organized the Natal Indian Congress.
- In the Dreyfus Affair, Alfred Dreyfus was convicted of treason.
- Coca-Cola was first manufactured in bottles.

There shall by no means enter [New Jerusalem] anything
that defiles, or causes an abomination or a lie,
but only those who are written in the Lamb's Book of Life.
REVELATION 21:27 NKJV

YOUNG MEN'S CHRISTIAN ASSOCIATION (YMCA)

Who works ten to twelve hours a day, six days a week? That's right, a workaholic—or the farm boys of nineteenth-century England who flocked to London to work in factories and mills. Far from home, they bunked together in their employers' crowded dormitories, or drifted into the city's tenements. Conditions stank—literally.

In 1844, George Williams, a draper (department store clerk) and a group of associates organized the first Young Men's Christian Association to enrich the lives of London's young workers. The first Y focused on Bible study, prayer, and fellowship.

> Fact: The founders of the YMCA welcomed boys of all Christian denominations and social classes, a revolutionary idea at the time when denominations and social classes rarely mixed socially.

By the early 1850s, Ys had spread throughout Great Britain and were well established in the United States and abroad. Ys thrived as religious and social centers and residences for young men. In the early twentieth century, influenced by evangelist Dwight L. Moody and others, YMCAs sent thousands of missionaries and workers overseas. The Great Depression of the 1930s, however, saw a dramatic downturn in the fortunes of YMCAs. Membership and donations dropped, and many of the Y's social services were rendered redundant by government programs.

Even more devastating was the "Great Delusion" of the 1960s and '70s. Reaction to the Vietnam War, the disgrace of President

Nixon's resignation, the assassination of political leaders, and widespread rebellion among the nation's youth lumped the YMCA together with all institutions to be distrusted. Yet winds shifted in the early 1980s. Interest in healthy lifestyles and wholesome values made people look again at the YMCA. Ys wisely refocused to meet current needs, and today offer a wide range of activities, pastimes, classes, and mentorship programs for all.

In the year 1844. . .
• Oscar I ruled as king of both Sweden and Norway.
• Samuel Morse sent the first telegraphic message.
• Charles Goodyear patented his method of strengthening rubber called vulcanization.

No discipline seems pleasant at the time, but painful.
Later on, however, it produces a harvest of righteousness
and peace for those who have been trained by it.
HEBREWS 12:11

WILLIAM WILBERFORCE

(1759–1833)
British Abolitionist

History recognizes William Wilberforce as one of the key figures of influence in the Western world. However, his early life did not reflect morality or seriousness in his studies. While a student at Cambridge, he would spend late nights playing cards, gambling, and drinking alcohol. Though he didn't apply himself to his education, at Cambridge he made a lifelong friend—William Pitt, the future prime minister of England.

During his first year as a member of Parliament, Wilberforce did very little. His own distinction was his pride and joy. Yet, as he reflected on his life over time, he began to regret his folly, abstain from alcohol, and turn back to his Christian faith.

Influenced by Thomas Clarkson, Wilberforce became obsessed with the abolition of slavery. He and Clarkson introduced twelve resolutions to Parliament against the slave trade, but all of them failed. Other bills over eight years were introduced and blocked primarily due to entrenched bigotry and political fear. Wilberforce began to write public essays on the topic, including "A Letter on the Abolition of the Slave Trade," which he used as the basis for the final phase of his campaign to Parliament. Finally in 1807, Parliament abolished slavery in the British Empire.

Fact: Wilberforce was a founding member of the Church Missionary, as well as the Society for the Prevention of Cruelty to Animals.

Wilberforce founded the African Institution, an organization dedicated to improving the lives of Africans living in the West

Indies. He supported efforts taking Christianity into West Africa. In declining health, he worked his remaining days to ensure that the measures passed were enforced.

In the year 1759. . .
• The Battle of Quebec was fought on the Plains of Abraham.
• Voltaire wrote the work *Candide*.
• Josiah Wedgwood founded Wedgewood Pottery Company.

It is for freedom that Christ has set us free. Stand firm, then, and do not let yourselves be burdened again by a yoke of slavery.
GALATIANS 5:1

Name Index

SCRIPTURE INDEX